Power of a Woman Series

Have You Walked in My Shoes?

Every woman walks a unique path.

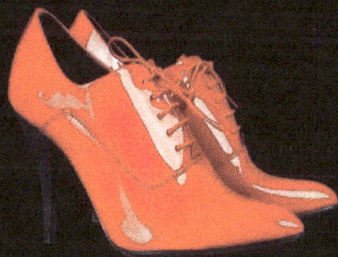

Dr. C. White-Elliott

This is a work of fiction combined with the Word of God. Any resemblance to actual occurrences is purely coincidental. Included scripture are from the King James Version of the Holy Bible.

CLF Publishing, LLC.
www.clfpublishing.org
909.315.3161

Cover design by Senir Design. Contact information: info@senirdesign.com.

ISBN # 978-1-945102-41-7

Printed in the United States of America.

Dedications

To my good friend Shelia, you are like a sister to me.
You are my travel partner (other than my husband, of
course). We will travel the world together!
And, you are an amazing Woman of God.

To my cousin Millicent, who is closer than blood.
We have created many memories over the years,
and our bond grows tighter by the day.

Acknowledgements

My heart goes out to every woman who has suffered ridicule, backbiting, envy, strife, and slander in the church and in the world at large. Those negative spirits serve to break down homes, communication, relationships, and even the Church (the body of Christ).

It is my prayer that after this book reaches the masses, a change will come about in the heart and minds of women everywhere (because women make up 70% of most churches).

Once this issue is overcome, we can move forward and focus on what God has called us to do- build His kingdom- and do it in the *true* spirit of unity.

Introduction

Women of God, it is time to pull the layers back and expose the enemy for the games he has been playing with us all. Yes, all of us! We have bought into the devil's shenanigans. We have formed teams and played the game. We have _all_ been guilty of the subject matter of this book at one time or another, whether we articulated our opinions to another person or whether we had thoughts running rampantly or either momentarily through our minds. Furthermore, some of us have been involved in the game more frequently than others, but frankly that is irrelevant. What is of the utmost importance is that we put a stop to it and show the enemy for the liar he is. Through this book, I am declaring a cease and desist!

Now, I can hear you asking, "What am I guilty of?"

Here it is: At some point in our lives, we have been guilty of judging another woman by her appearance, her hairstyle, her choice of dress, her diction, the tone of her voice, the sway of her hips, the size of her hips, her marital status, the supposed size of her bank account, her personality, her choice in men, her extracurricular activities, her educational level, etc.

Whether we want to admit it or not, our judgment stemmed from our own insecurities, jealousy, envy, low self-esteem, and an overall lack of love for our fellow woman. Whether this act on our part is a one-time offense or ongoing, whether it occurs when we are young and foolish or if it happens when we are old and foolish, the problem is- it continues to be perpetuated. It is a never-ending saga that can actually come to an immediate end, if we are willing.

But, here is the reality. In order for the cease and desist to actually be effective, the following question needs to be asked and answered: **What gives one woman the right to stand in judgment of another when she has not walked in the other woman's shoes?**

What exactly do I mean by that? It's simple!

Each woman has been traversing her individual journey from the day she was born, with a unique **set of circumstances** that has occurred and will occur only to and with her and her alone. Caution- I'm not saying she has experienced or will experience situations and occurrences that no one else has or will. *No.* What I am saying is the **sum total** of her experiences are completely different from the sum total of experiences of any other woman.

Wait! There is more. The sum total of experiences has shaped the woman into the person she is today. Those experiences have shaped her thoughts, her behaviors, her personality, her attitude, her diction, her decision-making process, her EVERYTHING.

Even she- who is a believer, who knows she is to cast down every imagination and high thing that attempts to exalt itself against the knowledge of God (II Corinthians 10:5), who works diligently to be transformed by the renewing of her mind to be not conformed to this world (Romans 12:2), who asks God to order her steps (Psalm 37:23), who strives to love her neighbor (Matthew 22:39) and esteem others higher than herself (Philippians 2:3), who gives charity while exhibiting the fruit of the Spirit (Galatians 5:22-23), who presses toward the mark for the prize of the high calling of God in Christ Jesus (Philippians 3:14-15), she, who does all of this, is yet in the process of sanctification, while trying to get to know and accept herself with all her shortcomings. The last thing she needs is for another woman to come up against her.

To *fully* understand her is to be her. To be her means to embody each and every experience she has ever had. Unless we can do that, allowing full under-standing to grace our finite minds, we need to refrain from passing judgment on another woman because we can never fully understand her plight. We can empathize and sympathize, but full and complete understanding will never manifest itself (unless the Holy Spirit intervenes).

Side note- When I stated we should refrain from judgment, I am not talking about loving judgment that is done to aide someone in her spiritual walk. I am referring to criticism that is done to inflict harm by tearing one down with backbiting and slander.

This, Women of God, is where the line should be drawn. For, we **are** Women of God, and we must learn to treat one another better. I am not saying we will like all the woman we encounter, but we can definitely love them and walk with them through the growing pains. We must begin to show the same love and understanding to others that we expect from them, for we are to love our neighbors as we love ourselves (Matthew 22:39).

Now, ask yourself this question, "How can we be effective in the work of ministry when jealousy, back-biting, envy, strife and jealousy continuously run rampant in the church?" The answer is, "We can't. We render ourselves ineffective when destructive spirits, mindsets, attitudes, and behaviors are present instead of the fruit of the spirit: love, joy, peace, longsuffering, gentleness, goodness, faith, meekness, and temperance (Galatians 5:22-23). We must place our complete focus on the gospel and the needs of people. Once we do that, the Church (as a whole) will be effective.

Finally, Proverbs 27:17 says, *"Iron sharpens iron."* Let's sharpen one another, as we walk through each trial together. If we concentrate our energy on shar-pening – fine tuning – one another and not focusing on perceived deficits, we will be stronger as the body of Christ, for there is strength in numbers. One of us can put 1,000 demons to flight, and two can put 10,000 to flight (Deuteronomy 32:30). Imagine what an entire army of us can do!

Together, we stand! Divided, we fall!

Read the following account of two women and see how a misstep could lead to a potential avalanche.

Chapter One

Melody Prentice was born to Janice, who at that moment became a single mother, who would raise her daughter in a one-parent household, due to Melody's father being absent from both their lives. Four years after Melody was born, Janice gave birth to a second child, Brian. Despite the absence of a father figure in the home and in Melody's life in general, she never felt unloved or neglected. Janice loved her two children with her whole heart and doted upon them. She worked hard to ensure they were well cared for financially, attending to their physical needs while never neglecting a single emotional need that arose. Under her mother's watchful eye, Melody grew up with confidence, security, and a healthy self-esteem.

During Melody's formative years, from age four to seventeen, she attended the local public schools in her area from kindergarten until she graduated from senior high. Although she struggled in a couple of her high school courses due to her lack of fully understanding the subject matter and the lack of a tutor, she was a model student with a 3.6 GPA, never failing a single course.

Aside from doing well academically, Melody was involved in sports: track and volleyball, making her a well-rounded student who was physically and mentally astute. Melody's outgoing personality made her a magnet for like personalities, leading her onto the path of popularity at an early age. She had so many friends that her life was never a dull moment, from elementary school throughout college. Melody was always busy with extracurricular activities from Monday through Saturday. So much so, Janice had a hard time keeping up with her daughter's schedule, as it shifted from one week to the next. The only constant was Melody staying busy, always having somewhere to be after school or early Saturday mornings. Nevertheless, Janice did her best to stay in the loop, so she could chauffeur or make sure her daughter had adequate transportation, which usually consisted of another parent being the chauffeur for the day.

In keeping up with the hype of the current high school fashion trends, Janice allowed Melody to shop for herself, with a preset budget of course. Melody always opted for name brand items and the latest fashions. That kept her as one of the fashionistas at her school. Although Melody had offered to get a part-time job after school, Janice would not hear of it because she wanted her daughter to give all of her attention to her academics and sports. She would not allow Melody to sacrifice her teenage years. If anyone would sacrifice, Janice determined it would be her. After all, she had decided to bring her children into this world, and she would do all she could to ensure they did not suffer unduly because of her choice.

Although Melody loved to be surrounded by her friends, high school was not all fun and games. That period of her life opened her eyes to many new opportunities and showed her aspects of her personality that had not yet been revealed to her. During her first internship at a local hospital, in which she participated during her eleventh-grade year, Melody discovered she was happiest when she cared for the sick, particularly infants and geriatrics. To her surprise, her inner calmness became disturbed when she witnessed a person in a debilitating condition. As soon as an afflicted person crossed or entered her line of sight, her heart leapt, and when she could, she rushed to the person's aide. The new discovery guided Melody's path from that moment forward.

After that first internship, Melody committed herself to two more before she graduated. Before making her final decision regarding her career choice, she wanted to be certain about her direction and not decide on a whim. Prior to discovering her passion for patient care, she had thought she would be a designer, which had stemmed from her love of fashion. As a matter of fact, she had already begun designing.

In her tenth-grade year, she had drawn sketches of dresses for several of her schoolmates who were planning to attend that year's prom or homecoming dance. With sketch in hand, each young lady went to a seamstress of her choice to have her dream dress created, and it all started with meeting Melody at a lunch table and describing the dress to her, from the design of the neckline, to the desired length, color, and style. When Melody and her clients attended the dances, their favorite pastime was ragging on the girls with store-bought dresses.

After completing all three internships at two different hospitals and after designing dresses for several young ladies at her high school, another high school and two private schools, Melody weighed her options carefully and finally decided on a career in healthcare. Although she loved seeing the excitement in the young girls' eyes when each one saw her finished sketch, nothing could replace the feeling of assisting in someone's care, especially if that person had no one else to visit or care for him/her. Melody liked filling someone's void, and she liked knowing she was making a real difference in the world.

Once Melody graduated high school, she enrolled in the local state college to study nursing. Although she loved the social scene and casual dating and could be found at a party and other types of social gatherings at least once a month, she was dedicated to her studies. Thus, to ensure each assignment, essay, and group project was submitted to her professors on time, Melody could be found in the school's library at least four days a week. She had found she could study for uninterrupted hours there versus having the constant interruptions that occurred at her apartment because her neighbors were constantly dropping in whenever they saw her or her roommate's car in the parking structure. Some of her neighbors were also college students, but they never seemed to study or complete homework assignments. All they wanted to talk about was the next party or who was dating whom. Her apartment complex felt more like a large coed fraternity/sorority house than an apartment complex.

Regardless of what was occurring on campus or in the complex, Melody would not attend any extracurricular activities until every assignment that was due in a two-week time frame was completed. One time and one time only had she broken her personal commitment, and she paid dearly for it. She had learned her lesson and vowed to never repeat the same mistake. Classmates were dropping out every semester. Melody did not want to be the next statistic. She had a goal to reach, and she was determined to accomplish it.

After four years of taking a full load of courses each semester, studying long hours, and completing two internships, on a beautiful Saturday morning, Melody proudly walked across the plush green lawn to the stage with her peers. Before stepping onto the stage, Melody took a quick glance toward the audience to ensure her mother, brother, grand-parents, other family members, and friends had their eyes on her. They did, so she gave them a quick wave. Finally, the moment she had been waiting for, from the moment she had enrolled in her first class, was coming to pass. Her heart leaped with pure joy, and her eyes moistened. Her hard work and dedication had paid off. When she heard her name called, her heart beamed with pride as she walked across the stage and gave a firm handshake to the university's president.

One week after Melody's graduation and all the festivities, she was packing her suitcase preparing for the luxurious trip she and her roommate would take to the Caribbean. Her roommate Jillian, whose name Melody frequently shortened to Jill, had graduated also, and they were both looking forward to time away on the beautiful island of Jamaica.

But as usual, Melody had not forsaken taking care of business prior to booking the trip, which her mother and grandparents gladly helped to pay for as a token of the pride they felt regarding her accomplishment. To make sure she was ready to enter the workforce in her chosen profession, one month before graduation, Melody had begun to interview. As an answered prayer, she was given an offer of employment from a prestigious hospital, which is well-known nationally, as well as a lesser-known hospital that has an impeccable reputation. Making the choice was difficult for Melody at first. However, knowing she was unsure if she would continue to live in her local geographical area, she opted for the prestigious hospital because of its numerous locations throughout the United States, knowing it would be easier to transfer within an organization versus from one organization to another.

When she accepted the offer, she did not hesitate to ask how soon she would be expected to report for work. Her question was answered with a follow-up question, "Will three to four weeks after graduation work for you? We do need to wait to obtain the fingerprint results and background report from the Department of Justice. Also, your educational institution has to confer your degree. We should receive those items within three to four weeks."

The response was music to Melody's ears. Although she was very excited to begin her long-awaited career, she really needed a breather. Her courses and internships had taken a toll on her, not to mention working part time to pay for personal expenses in the midst of it all. Her response to her employer's query was, "How about I plan to report July first?" After glancing at the calendar, her new employer answered, "Yes, that will suffice. Sounds like an excellent plan." From the date of graduation in late May to July first, Melody would have just over a month to herself to clear her head and get mentally prepared for her new job.

Eight days after graduation, Melody and Jillian found themselves relaxing on the beach, enjoying the soft, white sand between their toes, as the wind blew their thin sundresses about their legs. The fog that had filled their minds during the last few months as they brought their four-year course of study to a close had begun to lift. They no longer had to worry about essays, deadlines, time constraints, labs, or nosy neighbors.

Instead, they were free to thoroughly enjoy the resort that would be their home-away-from-home for the next six days. They had even turned off their cell phones and left them in their room. They didn't need to make calls to be entertained. They were too busy comparing one women's swimsuit to another's and discussing who was overweight and so on.

By the time July first came around, Melody was more than ready to go to work. She thought she needed all of the time she had allotted to clear her mind for her new job. As she found out, a week before the trip and one week after was a sufficient amount of time to clear her mind.

Arriving the first day, Melody felt completely at home. Having interned at that particular hospital twice did not hurt her comfort level either. She quickly learned the ropes and settled in.

For years, she enjoyed working as a registered nurse (a nurse practitioner), but she soon found interest in becoming a nurse supervisor, serving directly under the director of nursing. Already having secured the bachelor's degree and serving as a RN, she qualified for the job. When the position became available, she secured the job.

A few years later, the current director was preparing for retirement. There were several supervisors who desired her position, Melody included. Rumors began to float around about who would get the job. Would it be the one who had the highest seniority? Would it be the one with the best rapport with her staff of registered nurses and licensed vocational nurses? Would it be someone from outside the hospital? Would the Chief Nursing Officer and the hospital's CEO decide to hire a male this time around instead of a female? No one had a clue about what to expect, and all who wanted the position were truly walking around on pins and needles, seemingly holding their breath.

The only thing they could do was apply for the position, submit reference letters, interview, and hope for the best. So, Melody planned to do just that when the job posted. There were still a few months to go before the job became "live." Meanwhile, Melody would keep her eyes and ears open for any pointers that may come her way. She hoped her nerves would not get the best of her. Every time she thought about the possibility, her heart began to beat fast. But, as it would turn out, that was the least of her concerns.

Chapter Two

Tamara Hartford was born to her loving parents, Jackson and Samantha, who are still married today. Her parents, who are consummate professionals, love their only child immensely, but they had never planned to have children, so Tamara's arrival was unexpected to say the least. It wasn't that they did not want to have children. Jackson had been involved in an accident when he was an award-winning cyclist while still in college. Upon his discharge from the hospital, the attending physician told him he would more than likely not be able to have offspring of his own. So, he accepted the news as his reality, not bothering to get a second opinion.

When Jackson had begun to date Samantha, he explained his situation to her. She had already decided children were not a necessary part of her future, so she had no objections about entering into a relationship with him. Being on the same page as far as children were concerned, eventually the two married and advanced in their respective careers.

Then, nearly a decade later, taking the couple completely by surprise, Samantha awakened with morning sickness. She brushed it off, thinking she had caught a bug while overseas. However, the morning sickness persisted for another two weeks off and on. One of Samantha's girlfriends was finally able to persuade her to go to the doctor. When, the doctor delivered the shocking news of her pregnancy, she sat on the observation table with a blank look on her face. That was the last thing she had expected to hear.

Without a word, she took her cell phone from her handbag and dialed her husband's number. The physician left the room to give her some privacy. Calmly, she explained to her husband the results of her test, and the other end of the line fell quiet. Taking the lead, she asked Jackson if he was upset. In almost a whisper, he said, "Of course not. I have always wanted children. I just thought I would never have any. So, the question is, 'Are you upset?'" His wife pondered for a moment as she released the breath she had been holding. Softly, Samantha assured him that she was happy as well, honored to have his child.

Seven and a half months later, when Tamara was born, she was welcomed with open arms by both her parents and both sets of grandparents. The first five years of her life were just as routine as any other child who lived in her neighborhood. During those five years, from Monday through Friday, while her parents worked, Tamara was either with one set of her grandparents or the other. When her grandparents were unavailable, her parents called in the nanny to stay with Tamara during the day or on the evenings they had business meetings or dinner out with friends.

By the time Tamara came of age to attend first grade, her parents promptly filled her new set of luggage with clothes, toiletries and other personal items and sent her to the best boarding school money could provide. So, the time she spent with her parents and with her grandparents was greatly reduced. This saddened Tamara, and she left for boarding school with a heavy heart. She was accustomed to only seeing her parents in the evenings and on weekends, but she could not imagine only seeing them once a month for a weekend visit.

When they did come to visit or when they sent a car for her to come home, she was always very sullen. Most times, she would retreat to her bedroom. She was accustomed to being alone because at school, most of her time was spent in her room or in the library. When the other students attended social hour, she avoided being present. From the moment she had arrived, she had been treated as an outcast because she was the only new kid to begin that year, and it seemed as though ridiculing her was her classmates' favorite pastime. Being of mixed ancestry did not help either. The other girls found her to be peculiar, so they ridiculed her on a regular basis. They were either Asian, African American or of European descent. None of them were a mix of African and European ancestry.

Her parents did not really know how to deal with Tamara's mood and thought she would grow to love the boarding school. After all, they had both attended boarding school from ages six to fourteen before they attended a private high school that was much closer to home. They tried talking to her, but she refused to open up to them and share her feelings. She really did not believe they would understand her predi-cament, having never experienced it themselves. Over time, they came accustomed to their daughter's behavior pattern and chalked it up to adolescent growing pains.

By the time Tamara was in fifth grade, five years later, her parents noticed she was almost completely out of her shell. From the first time Tamara arrived to the school, on several occasions she had heard some of the teachers discussing a debate team. Tamara was intrigued and wanted an opportunity to participate in intellectual discussions although she would not have phrased it that way herself, seeing she was only eight and nine years old at the time her interest was developing. However, the debate team was only open to those in fifth grade and up. When the opportunity came for Tamara to join the team, she did not hesitate to apply.

One of the criteria for joining the debate team was earning good grades, and by good grades, the school required a 4.0 GPA. The second criterion was personal involvement in community service. Tamara qualified easily, as her GPA was 4.3, and she had volunteered weekly at a senior citizen home for the past six months, which was another way of escape for her from the girls who made her feel uncomfortable in her own skin. She was unsure of where the desire of their ridicule came from.

Like them, she was well groomed. Unlike them, she had not elected to wear makeup. She had flawless skin, and she preferred to allow her natural beauty to show, even when others acted as though she lacked in that area. Despite the negative reaction she received from others, Tamara knew who she was inside and out, and she was not easily swayed by another person's opinion, and she refrained from joining in the ridicule of other students.

Thirdly, each applicant was required to submit a position paper on a non-disclosed topic. The topic was not given until all applications had been received by the committee. After collecting the applications, each applicant was given a separate question, which was required to be answered by addressing both sides of the issue in a five-page essay. The applicants had one week to respond to the question and submit via an online forum.

Tamara, loving to engage in sound reasoning based on research, completed her essay the day after she received the question. After reading her essay three times and only making minimal changes, she submitted her essay immediately. It wasn't that she expected to earn brownie points by submitting early. She just didn't have any more to say on the topic and nothing to take from what she had already stated.

After the committee reviewed all the applications, they were tasked with choosing a team of five debaters and two alternates. Tamara was chosen to be one of the primary team of five. She was very excited and could not wait to share the news with her parents.

That weekend when Tamara left school to go home for a holiday weekend, she was so excited to be able to sit at the table with her entire family. On the drive in the town car with the hired driver, she planned exactly how she would break the news to them over dinner. She could imagine the looks of surprise that would cover the faces of those sitting around the table because Tamara did not always engage in in-depth conversations. It wasn't that she was timid; she just did not have anyone with whom she desired to engage deeply in a discussion. Her parents were certainly intellectuals, but they did not yet see her that way.

That Saturday evening, the caterers were in position, and the family had all arrived for the pre-planned Labor Day dinner. It was customary that each person would share any new projects, developments, or exciting news that was occurring in his/her life that had not already been previously shared with every-one. Anxiously, Tamara awaited her turn.

After listening to her grandparents, aunts, uncles, and a cousin or two, Tamara felt as though she was about to burst at the seams. When her turn came, she slid her chair back from the table and stood. Her parents looked at each other, and her grandparents looked at her parents. All of them had looks of puzzlement on their faces.

Before Tamara could speak, one of her cousins asked, "Tam, what is wrong with you? Why are you being so dramatic?" The cousin's mother tapped the girl on the leg, signaling for her to be quiet.

Tamara, with a huge smile covering her face, shared her news: "I was selected by a panel of ten to represent my school on the debate team."

For a moment the room was quiet. Tamara began to shift on her feet, as she moved her glasses around on her nose, wondering if she should have shared. Then, seemingly out of nowhere, everyone began clapping and saying how proud of Tamara they were. Someone asked, "Are you going to be nervous?" Tamara grinned, shook her head, and retook her seat. "No, I've been waiting a few years for this oppor-tunity."

For the next four years, Tamara remained on the debate team, and each year, her rhetorical skills were strengthened. When her teammates' interest would shift, causing them to leave the team, she would continue to remain dedicated. Over time, she began to participate in training new debaters, alongside the adult staff members.

When Tamara was in the eighth grade, something sparked her interest. When her high school debate team traveled to other locations for the debates, she began to notice that it wasn't always the debate team captain who introduced the team members. Sometimes, it was the student body president. Tamara begin to wonder why her school didn't have a student-run governance board.

One Monday afternoon, she spoke to her history teacher about her concern. Then, after a lengthy discussion that took place over four lunch periods between Tamara and her history teacher, Tamara decided to take her concern to the school administrator, Mrs. Hall. After listening to Tamara's spiel for approximately eight minutes, Mrs. Hall nodded her head and stated, "You have valid concerns and good reasoning, Miss Tamara. You are not the first student to raise this concern during the twelve years I have been here. However, the manner in which you have articulated your concerns is very impressive. I can see why you are debate team captain."

Tamara gave a slight smile as she listened, but she was waiting to hear a hint that her request would at least be considered. Mrs. Hall took a slight pause, fully expecting Tamara to jump in as most tweens would have done, demonstrating their pubescent angst. To her surprise, Tamara did not speak. Instead, she exhibiting great control over her personal energy. Mrs. Hall became further impressed with Tamara as a person. In the six and a half years that Tamara had been enrolled, Mrs. Hall had never spoken to Tamara outside the presence of her parents or one of her teachers.

Breaking the momentary silence, Mrs. Hall asked, "Miss Tamara, there is a staff meeting scheduled for next week. I will place your idea of a student council on the agenda. If a consensus can be reached and the administration decides to move forward, would you be willing to run for a position?"

Without hesitation, Tamara answered, "I plan to run for student body president. I already have my campaign speech ready. I would have never approached you with the idea if I were not planning to participate."

Slightly caught off guard by Tamara's response, Mrs. Hall asked, "I appreciate your enthusiasm, but are you telling me you have already written a speech – even without knowing what the decision of the administration would be?"

"No, of course not," Tamara answered with a slight tone of irritation. "The elements of the speech are in my mind and heart." Mrs. Hall nodded her under-standing and felt a little silly for asking when she noted Tamara's irritation.

After the administration voted for the students to have a governing council, Tamara ran for student body president and won easily. She was the only contender because no one wanted to run against her.

The majority of those eligible to vote (grades six through eight) believed she was the best person for the job – even those who had ridiculed her in the past. The minority that called her ability into question did not dare to publicly voice its opinions. Tamara governed the student body with the assistance of the vice president for the remainder of her seventh-grade year and won again for her eighth-grade year.

After eight years at the boarding school, it was time for Tamara to transition to the private school that was located closer to home. The school had the same feeling of entitlement, and the students held the same level of snobbishness. Immediately, Tamara became involved in her same activities (debate and student government), as she kept her ears open for other intriguing opportunities.

By the time Tamara graduated high school, she had grown in popularity, gained a trustworthy group of friends, and shed her awkward appearance which was mainly due to her dark rimmed glasses and wearing her hair in a bun at the nape of her neck. Her mixed heritage had always given her an exotic look, but Tamara had kept it masked. Now, she opted for contacts and always wore her naturally wavy hair loose, hanging down to the middle of her back.

Her verbal tenacity awakened her inner beast to its fullest capacity, and as she debated the given topics for the debate team and for the interest of the student body, she also spoke up for the underdogs on campus to any individual or a group of individuals that partook in harassing others. If the person or group attempted to ignore her, she forced him/her/the group to listen.

After graduating high school, Tamara attended the only school she applied to: Harvard. Her major was political science. After earning her B.A., she continued at Harvard, enrolling in its the law school. Three years later, she left Harvard with her jurist doctorate and an offer of employment at a law firm. As she began her employment, which was fully contingent upon her passing the bar, she studied for the exam. Six months later, on her first attempt, she passed.

Although Tamara had imagined herself as a lawyer for many years and she loved what she did, she knew she would not remain as a fully practicing one for very long. She had her eyes set on a higher position, one that would allow her to assist a greater number of people on a much larger scale. So, after practicing corporate law for eight years, Tamara was able to get herself elected to the United States Senate.

Chapter Three

Tamara walked out of the Senate chamber in Washington, D.C. at 4:39pm on a Friday evening after spending four straight hours deliberating on the upcoming Senate bills that would be placed on the ballot for the next election. Of the 100 United States senators, ninety-eight had been present, and they were all mentally and physically exhausted after the lengthy discussions. Normally, at the close of a three or four-day meeting, the majority of them would head to the Ronald Reagan Airport, Dulles International Airport, or Thurgood Marshall International Airport to catch a flight back to their home state where their families were anticipating their return.

For this trip, however, Tamara's plans were slightly different. Rather than return home that night, she would catch an early Sunday morning flight. For her, there was no particular rush to get home because at that moment, she was still husbandless and childless. And, that could remain a constant in her life for years to come. Frankly, she had not given it too much consideration. Her role in the Senate kept her far too busy to have time for a personal life or even a family. Others had managed to make it work, but Tamara wasn't there yet.

Her parents, on the other hand, had been hoping she would make a love connection with a fellow senator and take holy vows and not too long afterwards give them at least one grandchild. They had even gone as far as to mention their desires to Tamara on an occasion or two. Tamara would always smile and hear them out. Then, she would respond by telling them she was content with the current condition of her life and if anything were to change, they would be the first to know.

Unbeknownst to them, she had been dating the same man for just over a year. She would not call it a match made in heaven nor did she foresee a long life together for the two of them. She was quite confident he felt the same way although they had not actually discussed their future one way or the other. She needed someone with more drive, more tenacity, and more fire. And, it was her speculation that he probably desired someone with a little less drive than Tamara. Although he admired her accomplishments, he always wanted her around more. She enjoyed his company as well, but her career required her to move around the country without restraint.

So, eventually, when Tamara had a sane moment, her year-long relationship would come to an end. She did not see any reason to prolong the inevitable. And, knowing from the start the relationship would be short-lived, Tamara had not bothered to mention it to either of her parents. She allowed them to continue believing she was completely single, and in a month or so, she would be.

After Tamara had made it to her hotel room, taken a thirty-minute nap, and refreshed herself with a shower, she chose an after-five dress and a pair sling back pumps to wear to the evening festivities. Taking her time to maneuver her hair up into a high bun and apply light makeup to her face, she slowly made her way to the elevator. Her body was still very tired, lacking even enough energy to be excited about the evening. As the elevator descended, she felt her body sway. She quickly grabbed the rail to steady herself. She felt as though she had too much alcohol to drink. But, she had not had anything to drink all day. As a matter of fact, Tamara had not had a drop of alcohol since her first year in college. So, experiencing a drunken stupor was not her problem. So, she counted the dizziness to be a result of the long hours she and her colleagues had spent deliberating over the last several days.

By the time the elevator doors opened, Tamara felt better, but not quite herself. For a passing moment, she thought about returning to her room. She truly did not feel up to going anywhere, and she was not sure if the high heels she was standing on would carry her. Then, she looked down at the gift bag she was carrying. She had promised Margo she would not miss her special evening. Margo was having a "45" birthday bash with only her fellow senators while they were all in one place. Of course, all of them would not attend, but as Margo had put it, "Let whosoever will!" This celebration was just a precursor to the party she would have with family and friends when she returned home the next day.

Making it safely outside the front entrance of the hotel, Tamara sat inside a Lyft car. Again, Tamara began to feel nauseous. She felt as though the contents of her stomach would ascend to her throat.

Maybe it's acid reflux, she thought. *The Mexican food we were served for lunch was a tad greasy*, she reasoned. Then, realizing it had been at least six hours since she had consumed lunch, she didn't believe the food was the cause of her problem. At the same time though, she had no other explanation.

When the Lyft car pulled up to the InterContinental Hotel, Tamara was relieved to get out. She had felt as though she was on a tugboat in the middle of the Atlantic Ocean with waves beating on all sides of it. Slowly, she made her way into the hotel and to the Grand Ballroom. After greeting a few people briefly, she found the nearest table with an empty seat and placed herself into it. Then, she inconspicuously searched the table for a napkin. Spotting one, she retrieved it and removed the perspiration from her forehead.

Margo spotted Tamara and made her way to the table where she was sitting. Taking one look at her, Margo asked, "Are you okay, Tam?" Tamara gave a weak nod, but Margo was not convinced. Without questioning Tamara further, Margo said, "Let me get you a ginger ale." Tamara attempted to protest, but Margo had already turned to leave, and a few of the senators seated at the table were looking quizzically in Tamara's direction. Tamara smiled and ignored their curious glances. "How is everyone this evening?" she asked to divert their attention. John answered, "I'm sure you can guess. Dog tired." Everyone broke into laughter. Tamara was happy for the distraction.

Margo walked back over with the ginger ale, and Tamara took small sips, unsure if she should be digesting anything at that moment. The others seemed to have forgotten about Tamara and her need for Ginger ale. They were all talking and laughing. Forty minutes later, dinner was ready, and the guests formed a line at the buffet to fill their plates with the delicious-smelling food. Cautiously, Tamara walked over to the gift table and sat her gift down before joining the others. She was still unsure of whether or not she should ingest anything, but she did not want to raise questions from her lack of eating.

An hour or so later, the music was at full tilt, and the crowd was drinking, dancing, and having a good time. A few hours before, everyone's exhaustion had been showing. Now, they were as energetic and youthful as could be. Tamara was feeling better and was on the dance floor having a great time as well. Then, the lights were being flicked on and off, signaling everyone's attention. The music stopped, and everyone grew quiet, so they would not miss what would occur next.

Margo walked onto the stage and began to thank everyone for sharing in her birthday celebration. The words she shared demonstrated just how touched she was by their presence. One by one, the guests began to share Margo's sentiments by telling her how much of a pleasure it is to work with her for the duration they had known her. Some of them told funny stories, causing everyone to roar with laughter. After listening and enjoying the stories, Tamara decided she would take the microphone next, as she thought about how she and Margo had come to be close friends. Just as she lifted her leg to take the first step up to the stage, her entire body felt like rubber, and she felt herself fall...

When Tamara came to, a paramedic was kneeling over her and another paramedic was standing near her feet. Her fellow senators were standing just a couple feet away, on both sides of her, with looks of concern covering their faces. The paramedic closest to her was holding smelling salt under her nose and was asking her how she felt. She said she felt nauseous, almost intoxicated.

"Have you had anything to drink tonight?" the paramedic asked, noticing a bar in the corner of the room.

"No, I don't drink," Tamara answered groggily and matter-of-factly at the same time.

"How long have you been feeling nauseous?" he asked, as he moved the smelling salt away, seeing he no longer needed it.

"Just since this evening around 5pm, when I awakened from my nap."

"Does your head hurt? I don't know if you bumped it when you fainted."

Instead of answering, Tamara lifted her arm, prepared to search her scalp for bumps and bruises. The paramedic touched her arm gently to prevent her from lifting it. He wanted her to remain still and calm. Tamara noticed movement on her left side. Someone was stepping toward them from the crowd. Tamara looked up to see Steve. "I caught her before she went completely down. She didn't hit her head or any other part of her body," he assured the paramedics. Tamara didn't respond; she only looked from Steve to the paramedic, awaiting his next question.

"Let's see if you can stand," the paramedic said.

"Should we remove her heels?" Margo asked, thinking bare feet would allow Tamara to be more steady.

"That sounds like a good idea," the paramedic responded. Margo removed Tamara's shoes, and the two paramedics placed a hand under each of Tamara's arms, assisting her to her feet. Once she was fully erect, the second paramedic asked Tamara three questions, allowing her time to respond after each one: "What is your full name?" "What year is it?" "Who is our current president?"

After Tamara answered all three questions, the first paramedic asked if she thought she could walk around. Without verbally responding, Tamara began taking short steps, testing her legs out. When the paramedics were sure their patient would not fall, they released their grips but remained close by. Tamara was able to balance herself and walk unassisted. Next, one paramedic asked the standard question, "Do you want us to take you to the local hospital for observation?" Tamara knew she needed to see a physician because something was definitely wrong with her, but she wanted to see her primary physician back home. She did not want to go to an unknown facility or see a doctor there in D.C. and then still need to see another one back home.

"No, thank you. I will see my primary physician in North Carolina when I return home on Sunday."

"Are you traveling alone?" the second paramedic asked with a touch of concern in her voice.

Before Tamara could respond affirmatively, Robert stepped over and said, "We're on the same flight. I'll be with her." Tamara nodded a polite 'Thank you' to Robert. The paramedics gave her a release of liability form to sign before they left just in case there was a follow-up incident to what had occurred that night. Shortly after, Tamara took a Lyft back to her hotel and went directly to bed.

Chapter Four

When the airplane landed in North Carolina, Tamara thanked Robert for switching his original assigned seat to the one next to hers to be nearby in the event she needed assistance or felt ill. Thankfully though, Tamara had not been aware of much of the flight because she had taken a sleep aide thirty minutes before takeoff. She had no desire to experience the nausea she had been overwhelmed with for the past three days. For her, being on a flight could cause nausea by itself. She couldn't imagine how the flight coupled with whatever her condition was could cause her to feel. Thankfully, the sleep aide allowed her body to relax during the three-hour flight.

Just before they landed, Robert nudged Tamara gently, and she awoke. She was grateful when the wheels of the plane touched the ground. Very gingerly, as though expecting something to occur, she made her way off the plane. Looking through the crowd, with Robert not too far behind, it did not take Tamara long to spot her father. When she first saw him, she noticed he was frantically looking for her. Knowing her condition, he wanted to make his way to her quickly. He did not want her to be alone for too long, but he did not need to worry. Robert, who was determined to not leave her unattended, was by her side.

When Robert saw Jackson, he saw the resemblance between Tamara and her father immediately. When Jackson saw Tamara walking in his direction, relief flooded his face. Then, he hesitated when he saw Robert walking next to his daughter. Tamara had mentioned one of her colleagues would be with her on the plane. However, Jackson didn't expect to see a man holding onto her arm. As a father, that caused his antennas to rise and his back to straighten.

Robert met Jackson with an open hand, ready to shake. Jackson took Robert's hand, held it firmly and shook, as he looked directly into Robert's eyes. He was trying to see if anything else was going on - in addition to Robert helping a colleague who was under the weather. Tamara made introductions and thanked Robert again. Robert took that as his cue to leave and told Tamara he would see her in D.C. at the next appointed time. With all the wind she could muster into her lungs, Tamara said, "You got it." As Robert walked away, Jackson gave his daughter a tight hug; then, he stepped back and asked, "Are you okay, darling?"

"Not really, Dad."

"Should we go right to the hospital?"

"No, take me home. I just want to lie down."

"Well, you know they have beds at the hospital, too," he encouraged.

"I know, Dad," Tamara started. "I just want to be..." Her voice trailed off as she grabbed her father's arm.

"I think that settles it. Let me have your bag, and we will be on our way." Tamara remained quiet and followed her father's lead. She knew there was no point in debating with him. Holding Tamara's elbow, Jackson led her from the terminal to his car. As they walked, Jackson recalled Robert walking with Tamara in the same manner. Suddenly, he had clarity. Maybe Tamara's condition was worse than he had anticipated.

Getting onto the interstate, Jackson pointed his car in the direction of the hospital. Tamara sighed deeply as she felt the waves begin in her head. "Where is Mom?" she managed to ask.

"She is home awaiting my phone call."

"Call her now... and have... her meet us," she said with labored breaths.

"Okay, darling. Just sit back. Try not to talk."

When Tamara opened her eyes again, she was being lifted from the car and placed onto a gurney. She tried to lift her head, but everything went dark again. She could hear voices surrounding her, but one was very familiar. At the sound of the voice, she felt the fear lift from her. The voice gave her a sense of calm. It was her mother's voice.

Then, another voice disturbed the calmness she was feeling in the midst of her dizziness. Someone was asking her, to consent to blood being taken. Tests needed to be run immediately, so answers could be provided for the cause of the symptoms Tamara had been experiencing for the last few days. Tamara consented to the test and motioned to her mother to be her voice. The nurse interpreted the gesture and asked, "Are you giving your mother permission to speak for you and make medical decisions?" Tamara nodded. "I need a verbal 'yes,' Ms. Hartford." No sooner than Tamara had responded, a needle was pushed into a vein in her arm, and blood was being drawn.

Tamara didn't have a problem with needles. However, she would have certainly appreciated being pre-warned prior to a needle being inserted into her arm. Through it all, she refrained from complaining. She definitely did not want to hinder the nurses from running all needed tests. Although she hadn't been there long, she was already looking forward to leaving and going home to sleep in her own comfy bed, which she had not slept in since the prior Monday night. In her mind, she could await the test results in the comfort of her home.

After having several vials of blood drawn and providing a urine sample, Tamara reclined on the stack of pillows and nodded off. Her parents left her to rest and walked down the corridor to the cafeteria. Neither of them had taken an opportunity to eat breakfast due to their concern for their daughter. A couple of hours later, when Tamara's physician Dr. Young became available, he went to her room. She had been moved from the emergency room to a private room. That was standard hospital procedure for all government officials at Tamara's level of clearance.

After asking Tamara what seemed to be an extended survey of questions, Dr. Young informed her she would not be released from the hospital that day. He was concerned about her symptoms and wanted to keep her for observation until her test results returned from the lab. His primary concern was the number of dizzy spells Tamara had experienced during the last 48-72 hours and the fact that she had never experienced any of the symptoms before. He did not want to risk her going home and passing out, causing injury to her physical person. Before leaving, he told her he would check with her first thing the next morning.

Tamara was disappointed to receive the news regarding her release, but she appreciated the doctor's concern and care for her wellbeing. So, with no other viable options, she reached for the remote and turned the television on. She did not regularly engage in watching television, but her options for other activities were nonexistent. She would have preferred surfing the internet, but her father had left her computer bag in his car. Not much later, her mother walked into her room alone.

"Looks like someone has made herself comfortable," Samantha said.

"No other choice. Dr. Young said I will be parked here overnight."

"Is it serious?" Samantha asked with concern, as she slowly lowered herself into a recliner that was positioned on the side of Tamara's bed.

"It's a precaution. No test results yet," Tamara said without looking at her mother. She continued to channel surf, looking for something interesting to watch. Her mother said nothing; she sat quietly observing her daughter who wasn't immune to holding information back from her. Ignoring her mother's perusal of her countenance, Tamara asked, "Where's Dad?" as she felt her mother's eyes crawl across her skin.

"He had to run an errand. He'll be back in an hour or so."

"By chance did he go downtown?" Tamara asked. Samantha smiled.

"As a matter of fact he did. Thinking about your favorite soup?" Tamara nodded. "I'll call him." Just as Samantha took out her cell phone to call her husband about Tamara's request, a nurse walked in. So, Samantha stepped into the hallway to make her call.

"Good afternoon, Senator Hartford. I am Melody Prentice. I am one of the nursing supervisors, and I understand my nurses have been taking very good care of you during the short time you have been with us. Is there anything we can get you?"

"No, thank you. I am doing okay for the time being."

"How are you feeling? Any sensations of dizziness or fatigue right now?"

"Actually, I am a little fatigued. It could be jetlag though," Tamara said, thinking wishfully.

"Okay, if you need anything, don't forget to press the button, and someone will come in from the nurses' station."

"Oh, there is one thing I need. May I have a bottle of water. My mouth is really dry."

"Sure. No problem. Let me grab that now."

Just as Melody walked out of the room, another nurse was walking in. They greeted each other as though they had not seen each other in a while, like sorority sisters who had lost contact. The second nurse, Tiffany, was there to check Tamara's vitals. When Melody arrived back to the room with the bottle of water, Tiffany had a cup and straw ready. Melody handed the bottle to Tiffany to pour into the cup. As Tiffany poured, she said, "I see the job opening you have been waiting for has finally posted."

Melody smiled broadly. "Yes, I saw it on the board this morning when I came in."

"Didn't you receive it in your email?"

"I haven't had a chance to check yet," Melody said as she pulled out her phone. She began scrolling through her email. "No, it's not here."

"Warren knows she is supposed to send it to everyone in the department who qualifies as well as post it outside the hospital. Do you think her not sending it has anything to do with the issue that arose last year?"

"I have no idea," Melody answered absent-mindedly, as she watched Tiffany work.

"I thought the two of you had gotten past the issue some time ago."

"Who knows what is going through her mind. I thought we had gotten past it too, but every time she passes me in the hallway, she looks the other way. She needs to take that stick out her..." Melody suddenly looked down at Tamara, as if though she forgot she was in the room with them. "We will check on you later, dear," Melody said to Tamara, while motioning to Tiffany that they should head towards the door. Trying to ignore them and their conversation, Tamara had finally found something worthwhile to watch on television, so she shifted her position in the bed to make herself more comfortable. She was surprised to hear Tiffany and Melody's voices right outside her door.

"Yeah, and she needs to get a makeover while she's having the stick removed." Tiffany laughed at her own comment, and Melody laughed right along with her. "Who do you think your biggest competition is for the position?"

"Competition! Yeah, right. If you really want to know the truth about it, there is no competition. I have the best record around here."

"So, you're saying you are going to get the job, hands down?" Tiffany challenged. Melody stood quietly for a moment.

"I'm saying I deserve the job based on my record. No one here has been here as long as I have nor did they start at the level I started at here. My record should speak for itself."

"What about Belinda? I heard her rep was pretty solid."

"Belinda, the new lady with the smug attitude, who will barely speak to anyone? I don't know much about her."

"Yes, that's the one. I'm just trying to get you to think about it. You seem pretty confident. Don't let being over confident blow your chance."

"I'm confident, yes. But, I'm not inflated. I'm realistic."

Right at that moment, a patient, Mrs. Templeton, was being wheeled out of her room by an orderly. She waved at the two nurses as she went by. Both of them waved back hesitantly. "Why is she waving at us as though she is the patient of the year? Every time she comes here, she is extremely rude to everyone on our floor. If her food is steaming hot, she yells. If her doctor is unavailable, she acts as though she is being mistreated. I'm glad she isn't my patient. I don't know what I would do with her," Melody said.

Tiffany responded, "Wasn't she your patient at one time?"

"Yes, but I had my supervisor at the time to switch her to another nurse."

"Why?"

"I just couldn't deal with her antics."

"Most patients have at least one antic or another," Tiffany said with annoyance in her voice. "So, you just passed her off to someone else?"

"Yeah," Melody said nonchalantly.

"Wow," Tiffany responded in disbelief before walking away to complete her rounds.

Tamara couldn't help overhearing the conversation the nurses had right outside her doorway. She shook her head slowly and focused on her television program, disappointed at how the two nurses were behaving, but particularly with Melody's disposition of not caring for all patients equally. From what she had understood, Melody was assigned a patient, but she decided the patient's behaviors were too much for her to bear.

While Tamara lay there and pondered her thoughts, her mother returned with the good news of Jackson bringing both of them a bowl of soup. Tamara could already taste it on her tongue.

Later that evening, Tamara got up from her bed to go to the restroom. Upon exiting the restroom, she heard voices near her door. She stepped into the doorway to see who was there. She saw Melody and another nurse at the nurses' station. She didn't realize when she was brought over from the emergency room that her room was right next to the nurses' station. That explained why earlier that afternoon she could hear Tiffany and Melody so easily.

When Melody noticed Tamara's presence, she asked, "Do you need something, Senator?" Tamara shook her head; then, she stated, "No, just coming from the restroom." By that time, the other nurse, Paul, had come over to the doorway. "Let me help you get back into bed." Samantha stood and said, "I can help her. Thank you."

Paul asked, "Are you sure? It's no problem."

"Thank you. We're okay," Samantha responded, as Tamara sat on the side of the bed, and Samantha lifted her legs onto the bed and placed the sheet over her daughter.

"Well, just ring if you need us," Paul said as he exited.

Not long after, Jackson and Samantha said good night and ensured Tamara they would both return in the morning. Tamara said, "But not too early," with a smile.

"We get the hint," her mother said.

"Rest well," her father added. They exited the room, leaving Tamara with her own thoughts. Feeling exhausted still, Tamara decided to turn off the television and get some rest. From the time she had been there, she had only napped off and on.

Turning the television off caused every sound to be magnified. The voices from the nurses' station seemed louder. Melody and Paul sounded as though they were standing in her doorway. Tamara was comfortable and did not want to get up to close the door. She decided she could just tune them out and fall asleep. Before her thought became a reality, she overheard Paul picking Melody's brain.

"So, Mel, it's widely known that you will be applying for the director position."

"Yeah, Paul. It's no secret."

Ignoring her sarcasm, Paul asked, "As director, what would you bring to the table? What would you institute? What changes would you make to better the department?"

"Why are you interviewing me?"

"Have you not considered these questions? If you do not anticipate making departmental changes, what is your interest in being a director?" he queried.

"Of course, I have."

"Look, from the buzz around here, there are at least four of you from inside our department who will apply for the position. Then, of course, there are others who will possible apply from outside. So, all I am saying is, you want to be competitive in your responses."

"Yes, I understand that."

"So, do you have any specific plans for how you would run the department? Are there any changes you would make?"

"Well, for one, I would pick up any issues our current director left undone, issues that I agree with of course."

"Such as?" Paul prodded.

"Such as the issue of parity that continues to come up every year or so."

"That's a start. Do you have a specific plan for tackling it?"

"Not just yet. You know, whatever I choose to do will be more than what the last one did."

"Actually, the director has accomplished many great feats in her seven years as director. Remember, she is retiring. She isn't being fired. So, no one is complaining about her job performance. So, comparing yourself to her is a moot point. The director before her was asked to step down and return to being a supervisor because he could not handle the workload. Are you prepared to work long hours doing what needs to be done?"

"Of course. And speaking of long hours, I will fight to get our hours reduced by hiring more nurses."

"Sounds good. Question..."

"Go ahead."

"Wasn't there an issue with you wanting to choose your patients and the nurses you supervised?"

"Yes, I did make special requests here and there. What's wrong with that?"

"It just shows that you are not willing to work with everyone and that you can't handle difficult patients."

Melody fell silent. She began to ponder on Paul's words. There was definitely some truth to what he was saying. As she sat thinking about his words, he said, "Good night," because his shift was ending.

When Tamara awoke the next morning, she could hear the hustle and bustle of patients in the hallway, moving here and there. As she began to lift herself from the bed to make her morning bathroom run, she felt a wave of nausea overcome her. She quickly reclined on her pillow, waiting for the moment to pass.

As she continued to lie there, catching her breath, Dr. Young walked in. "Good morning, Senator. Oh, you are not looking well."

"I'm not feeling well. I am very nauseas."

"I'm sure you are. According to your symptoms and test results, you are suffering from Vertigo, which is a sensation of whirling and loss of balance, caused by disease or infection affecting the inner ear or the vestibular nerve."

"I have heard of it before."

"So, now that we know what it is, we can look to treatments. The first thing we need to do is treat the inner ear infection you have and then deal with any reoccurrences of Vertigo that may come about as a result."

"Sounds good to me."

"Here are your prescriptions. This is for the infection, and the other two are to reduce the occurrences of Vertigo, so it won't knock you off your feet." They both laughed as Dr. Young handed the prescriptions to Tamara.

"Thank you, Dr. Young."

"You are welcome. It is good to see you. Unfortunate circumstances though. Anyway, the nurse will be in with your discharge papers shortly."

"Sounds good. I'm ready to go."

"Well, hold tight. It may be a few hours. So, try to get some rest."

Tamara decided to try again to see if she could make it to the restroom without passing out or falling. After she was done, she decided to sit in the chair near the doorway and call her mother to update her on the doctor's findings and to prepare her to come pick her up in a few hours.

After completing her phone call, Tamara grabbed her iPad and began to check her emails. She had received several from her fellow senators who were wishing her well and checking on her prognosis. Robert must have given them an update although none of them knew she had been taken to the hospital.

A half an hour later, Melody walked into Tamara's room. Melody wasn't her normal cheery self, as she had been the night before when she was in there with Tiffany.

"Good morning, Senator. How are you feeling?" Melody asked with a melancholy voice.

Tamara noticed her demeanor and answered, "I'm taking it slowly. Dr. Young stopped by and explained everything. I'm looking forward to go home. How are you? Is there something on your mind?"

"Why do you ask?"

"You just seem preoccupied," Tamara answered cautiously, not wanting to rub Melody the wrong way.

"Do you have a minute to talk? I mean, I don't want to disturb you if you're busy or not feeling well."

"Sure, I'm feeling okay. I'm not going anywhere," Tamara said with a smile, trying to make Melody comfortable. Tamara stood and sat on the bed, offering the only chair in the room to Melody.

Melody closed the door before she sat in the chair. Looking intently at Tamara, she asked, "Have you ever had a strong desire for something but felt as though you could not achieve it? As though there was something blocking you?"

"Sure," Tamara asked, waiting for Melody to continue.

"There is a position available that I plan to apply for. I have wanted this position for quite a while."

"Okay, and what do you believe is standing in your way?"

"I'm not sure, but I am glad it is not a position like yours where I have to be voted in. Unfortunately, there are some people who are not in my corner like I expected them to be."

"How do you know they are not in your corner? Have they said something?"

"Well, a few people have brought up past instances that they believe may be held against me during the hiring process."

Tamara speculated in her mind about where Melody was headed based on the conversations she had overhead on the previous day. However, she kept silent. When Melody did not add anything else, Tamara asked, "Can you give me an example?"

"Well, one person brought up the fact that I requested for one of my patients to be shifted to another nurse. He said that was bad judgment."

"How do you feel about your request?"

"At the time, I didn't see anything wrong with it. I thought maybe someone with a personality similar to the patient's could handle her better than I could."

"And how do you see the situation now?"

"Pretty much the same."

"And how does the person who brought it to your attention view the situation?"

"He said it shows that I prefer one type of patient over another and that I should be willing to work with all patients because they all need our attention and care."

"Do you not agree with that?"

"Well, when he put it that way, I guess I do agree."

"So, what is really the problem here?" Tamara asked.

"I'm wondering if others will see my interaction with patients and nurses the way some of my coworkers do. If they do, that may spoil my chances of getting the job."

"So, is the problem how others view you or is there an internal problem?"

"What do you mean?" Melody asked sincerely.

"Can I be frank with you?"

"Of course, Senator. You are a well-respected person, and you have made many important decisions for our state and for our country. I respect your opinion."

"Okay. Here goes. I overheard a few of your conversations yesterday." Before Tamara could continue, Melody's head dropped, but she did not utter a word. "Now, you seem like a person who is good at what she does…"

Melody interrupted her, "You don't have to sugar-coat anything you are about to say. I'm a big girl. I can handle it. Just let me have it straight."

"Your disposition toward other people appears to be very self-serving."

"What do you mean by that? Do you mean I have my own agenda?"

"Yes, that is exactly what I mean. One of your coworkers said you had transferred a patient who was in your care to another nurse, and from your own lips, I heard you say you were glad the patient wasn't your patient because you could not deal with her antics. Your coworker made a good point when she said everyone has antics. Think about it, there is a director of nursing, and he/she has to deal with the temperament of each nurse. The director doesn't get to pick and choose whom he/she deals with. Whichever supervisor and nurse is employed by this hospital, the director must supervise without prejudice."

Melody said nothing. As Tamara spoke, Melody nodded and took Tamara's words in.

Tamara continued, "Then, another coworker mentioned you essentially did the same thing when you became supervisor. You handpicked the nurses you wanted and left the supervision of the others to someone else. That act was selfish and self-serving as well. When you excluded some patients and fellow nurses, that placed them in a category of being unworthy of your attention, your friendship, and your guidance."

"I understand," Melody said with tears in her eyes.

"Also, you made derogatory comments about patients and coworkers. That was very unbecoming as a professional, as a woman, and as a human being. Instead of speaking ill to someone or about someone, you should be loving. You have chosen a career that helps people heal, but unfortunately, you don't seem to give the same attention to their emotional well-being. You do understand that our words can be harmful to others, don't you?"

"Yes, I do understand that. But, I never saw my-self as the type of person to use her words to hurt others. I'm ashamed to be having this conversation quite frankly."

"Melody, I understand your feelings of being disappointed. However, what would be more disa-ppointing is to remain in the same condition. The objective here is understanding your dilemma and working to overcome it. Listen, you are a loving person who was obviously moved to go into a career that is filled with loving and caring individuals who spend their lives seeing to the needs of others. Somewhere along the way, you became sidetracked and turned the attention onto yourself instead of those around you. Now, that you see the problem, do all you can to fix it."

"I can do that. It may take some time though, but I believe I can demonstrate my love for people rather than pointing out the things I don't particularly care for. You know, someone asked me what changes I would make for the department as director, and I didn't have a well-thought out answer. I believe I really wanted the position to make a name for myself, to further my own agenda."

"That's an honest statement. That is a good start."

"I have much soul searching to do. So, I don't believe I should submit an application for the director position. I don't think I am ready. I need to direct my attention to where it should be and not where it presently is."

Tamara stood from the bed, walked over to Melody and hugged her, as Melody cried softly.

Melody did not apply for the position, but she did begin to watch her comments and change her disposition toward others. She began to see what others had seen all along, but they had never bothered to mention it until a crucial moment in her life. Nevertheless, she was thankful because their words demonstrated their care and concern for her. For that, she was grateful. Their words and the attention she paid to those words helped her to make the right decision about applying for the director's job. With her present disposition, she was not ready to accept responsibility for directing an entire staff of nurses.

Melody was very successful in her job and in her personal life. However, she had a tendency to overlook other's feelings, feelings of patients and co-workers alike.

When we encounter someone life Melody or if we are someone like Melody, we need to do as she did-change our behaviors. After first, she wanted to point the finger to others, saying it was their mindset or perspective about her decisions. That is the response of many, placing the fault with others rather than taking responsibility for one's own actions. When we know better, we can do better.

Tamara was available to speak to Melody with love, telling her the truth, but not beating her down with it. Melody already felt bad enough, and Tamara wasn't there to exploit her feelings. Instead, she was there to lend an ear and give an honest assessment.

However, here is a word of caution- not everyone is going to respond as Melody did. Some will be belligerent, responding in a negative manner, not wanting to accept responsibility. When that occurs, we should leave the situation as calmly as possible. In due season, the person will take responsibility and the steps necessary to change her demeanor. All you can do after sharing your perceptions is pray. God will do the rest.

Chapter Five

The situation that was exemplified in the scenario of Melody and Tamara is nothing new in the relationship and demeanor of women around the world. As long as women have mouths and there is a lack of mutual respect for fellow women, there will be continued ridicule and disrespect flowing between women everywhere. Several occurrences in the Bible show this to be an age-old problem.

In this chapter, we will review several biblical examples of negative behavior and/or words and then examine at least one alternative response to each in order to understand and acknowledge there is always a more positive way to respond to negativity. If we are willing to extend an olive branch or a kind word or gesture to someone else, that could shed a positive light on the situation instead of creating further despair.

Scenario #1- Sarah and Hagar

In Abraham's old age, God promised him a son who would be an heir from his own bowels (Genesis 15:4). Up to that point, Abraham and his wife Sarah, had not conceived a child, and Abraham was concerned he would have no heir of his own and would need to leave all his earthly possessions to his servant Eliezer. Then, for years after the promise was given,

Sarah had still failed to conceive. So, we read in Genesis 16, Sarah speaking to Abraham, *"Behold now, the LORD hath restrained me from bearing: I pray thee, go in unto my maid; it may be that I may obtain children by her."* Hearkening unto the voice of his wife, Abraham slept with Hagar, Sarah's Egyptian handmaid.

Before we progress with Sarah's story, let us take a look at two things: 1) the relationship between Sarah and Hagar and 2) the Hebrew custom regarding the childbearing of slaves.

Regarding the relationship between Sarah and her handmaid Hagar not much is said. We are not provided much background information on Hagar at all. As a matter of fact, Hagar is not mentioned in the story of Abraham and Sarah until Genesis Chapter 16, when the issue concerning a rightful heir to Abraham's fortune comes up and Sarah seemingly has lost hope in conceiving a child even though God made the promise to her husband.

Hagar was Sarah's slave, so Hagar answered to Sarah and did her bidding. We can assume it was a relationship of respect being ushered from Hagar to her mistress Sarah and possibly vice versa. Whatever Sarah commanded or asked, Hagar did. That was the customary relationship between a slave and his/her owner.

Now, let's examine the tradition of childbearing as it relates to a slave and her owner that had been established in the Hebrew community. If a slave woman engages in intercourse with her male owner and becomes pregnant, the child she bears becomes the child of the man's wife, if his wife so desires. In the case of Sarah and Hagar, it was Sarah's sole intent for Hagar to bear a child for her because she was unable to bear a child of her own, and she desired for Abraham to have a son (Genesis 16:2). Without that specific need being present, Sarah would have never offered for her husband to engage with Hagar or any other woman.

After Hagar engaged with Abraham, she did indeed conceive. So, Sarah's plan was successful. Then, the unexpected occurred. The respect that was understood between Hagar and Sarah dissipated. Genesis 16:4 says, *"And he* [Abraham] *went in unto Hagar, and she conceived: and when she saw that she had conceived, her mistress* [Sarah] *was despised in her eyes."*

Having conceived of Abraham, something Sarah was unable to do, Hagar became haughty and began to look down upon Sarah. Hagar's attitude said to Sarah (in so many words), "I am better than you are. I was able to do what you were unable to do. Therefore, I am worth more in your husband's eyes than you." Sarah noticed the change in Hagar's disposition, and before reacting, she took the situation to her husband. Abraham told Sarah that Hagar is her handmaid, so she was free to deal with her as she wished. So, Sarah chose to deal with her harshly. Because of the disrespect Hagar demon-strated to Sarah, Sarah let her know she was still just a slave girl and not to forget her position.

Let's examine the problem here and ascertain how and why things went wrong. In their situation, one woman had need of another. Rather than offering the help that was needed (or completing the task with humility), the woman issuing the help (Hagar) began to believe herself to be superior to the one who could not *yet* accomplish the task (Sarah). The spirit of superiority creeped in, causing Hagar to despise Sarah, seeing her as beneath her or as not having the same level of worth because she was unable to produce a child for her husband. Their relationship became broken and remained so until Hagar finally left the camp years later with her and Abraham's son Ishmael.

The first problem was Sarah did not stand firm on her faith in God, being unwavering in her belief that God would fulfill His promise. The second problem was Sarah decided to take matters into her own hands to ensure her husband had the heir he desired. So, when she went to Hagar and requested her assistance, Hagar should have done the deed and kept her mouth closed. Problem three- Hagar did not do that. After she accomplished the task, she belittled Sarah. As a result, Sarah reacted- problem four.

Sarah was humiliated and that led her to respond improperly to Hagar. Even though Hagar was behaving immaturely about the situation, Sarah should have held her tongue and not reacted. Yes, I realize it is much easier said than done, especially when it comes to your spouse. Nevertheless, Sarah should have shown Hagar love. After all, Sarah herself created that situation. Hagar would have eventually understood that her place in that home had not changed regardless of what had transpired with the birth of her son. Sarah was yet worthy of Hagar's respect.

If both women would have dealt with one another with love and kindness, much of what occurred could have been prevented. But, haughty spirits got in the way and led to a broken family and disgruntled spirits. But, that is what happens when one is disobedient to God's Word.

Scenario #2- Peninnah and Hannah

Now, let's examine a similar situation involving the two wives of Elkanah. Elkanah was married to both Peninnah and Hannah. Peninnah had born children for Elkanah, while Hannah had not. As a result, the first issue ensued: Peninnah had a ritual of taunting Hannah on a regular basis because she was barren, causing her extreme remorse. *"And her adversary also provoked her sore, for to make her fret, because the Lord had shut up her womb"* (I Samuel 1:6). Hannah was so overcome with grief; she would not eat. She spent many days shedding tears and praying for God to open her womb and give her the gift of motherhood.

Rather than Peninnah taking pity on her sister wife and having empathy for her, understanding their situations could have been easily reversed, she held an air of superiority because the Lord had blessed her to bear children. Here, we see one woman (Peninnah) comparing her abilities to those of another woman (Hannah). This behavior demonstrates Peninnah's lack of understanding or care that God provided each of us with different abilities for different purposes. Not all women are able to accomplish the same tasks, even something that is taken for granted or viewed as automatic, such as bearing children. Because most women do produce offspring, children are not always viewed as blessings. Instead, they are viewed as a natural part of life. This mindset caused a breakdown in Peninnah and Hannah's relationship, if they ever had a healthy relationship to begin with.

Peninnah's behavior hurt Hannah to her core, but Peninnah held no regrets. It did not bother her at all that Hannah was in emotional turmoil. It was as though Peninnah took pleasure in causing Hannah distress. I wonder how Peninnah would have felt if the tables were turned.

In the midst of being mocked, Hannah prayed to the Lord that her womb would be opened, so she could conceive a child for her husband although he already had children from the womb of Peninnah. *"And she [Hannah] vowed a vow, and said, O Lord of hosts, if thou wilt indeed look on the affliction of thine handmaid, and remember me, and not forget thine handmaid, but wilt give unto thine handmaid a man child, then I will give him unto the Lord all the days of his life, and there shall no razor come upon his head"* (I Samuel 1:11).

As time went on, Hannah eventually conceived a child. *"Wherefore it came to pass, when the time was come about after Hannah had conceived, that she bare a son, and called his name Samuel, saying, Because I have asked him of the Lord"* (I Samuel 1:20). She was elated. Her prayers had been answered, and she would be able to enjoy the experience of childrearing.

Note- Nowhere in scripture is it recorded that Hannah returned the hatred her sister wife Peninnah had shown her. She kept a sweet spirit about herself at all times. She did not look for an opportunity to scheme and plan her retaliation upon Peninnah. She went about her way and walked in the blessings of the Lord. Instead of dealing with Peninnah harshly, she took her concerns and her sadness to the Lord and asked Him to change her circumstance, while vowing a vow of what she would do should He bless her.

As women of God, that is what we must do despite the behavior of others. We must return hatred, bitterness, jealously, envy, and strife with love. When we choose to retaliate or to fight fire with fire, we lose time, and we lose focus on the task at hand. Life is short and time is too precious to be overwhelmed by foolishness.

Let's switch gears and take a look at two positive biblical examples regarding women. These examples illustrate how women should interact with one another despite the trials we face and the difficulties we encounter. These examples also show us the temperament we should possess and the how to exhibit the nine fruit of the spirit: love, joy, peace, longsuffering, gentleness, goodness, faith, meekness, and temperance (Galatians 5:22-23) regardless of the situations we encounter.

Scenario #3- Elisabeth and Mary

The first example we will explore is the relationship of Elisabeth and Mary. At a young age, Mary was engaged to Joseph. During that time, she had a visitation by the angel Gabriel. The angel approached Mary saying, *"Fear not, Mary: for thou hast found favour with God. And, behold, thou shalt conceive in thy womb, and bring forth a son, and shalt call his name JESUS"* (Luke 1:30-31). Mary found his statement and the encounter odd, to say the least, because she was a virgin, having never known a man intimately. She wondered and asked how conceiving would be remotely possible without having ever engaged in intercourse. However, even with Mary's question, her faith caused her to respond in the following manner: *"Behold the handmaid of the Lord; be it unto me according to thy word"* (Luke 1:38). She trusted the Lord explicitly and whatever design or direction He had for her life, she would attend to His Word and watch Him perform it in her life. Mary was a young woman of great faith, and even this uncertainty for her was certain.

Once Mary had conceived her son, she left her home town in haste to go to the hill country in Juda, to visit her cousin Elisabeth, who had once been barren but was then with child. When Mary arrived, Elisabeth greeted her, and the baby Elisabeth carried in her womb leaped at Mary's presence (Luke 1:41). Then, Elisabeth was filled with the Holy Spirit.

Immediately, upon seeing her cousin, Elisabeth blessed Mary and encouraged her by saying, *"Blessed art thou among women, and blessed is the fruit of thy womb. And whence is this to me, that the mother of my Lord should come to me? For, lo, as soon as the voice of thy salutation sounded in mine ears, the babe leaped in my womb for joy. And blessed is she that believed: for there shall be a performance of those things which were told her from the Lord"* (Luke 1:42b-45).

With the love Elisabeth showed to her cousin Mary, Mary was able to stay in her home for three months. Elisabeth's home provided shelter for Mary for the harsh treatment she may have received from the inhabitants of her city- at least for the time being.

Elisabeth, on the other hand, did not treat her cousin unfairly or with scorn. Her faith and belief in God fortified her ability to love her cousin and to believe God had chosen Mary to bring forth the Messiah. Someone with a worldly spirit or weak faith or even no faith would have belittled Mary and scorned her for having a child out of wedlock. Elisabeth and Mary's relationship is the perfect example of sisterly love.

Without the moving of the Holy Spirit upon Elisabeth, it is possible she would have responded differently to Mary and her pregnancy. She may have even turned Mary away from her home, not wanting to deal with talk from her neighbors or the town's people. Most of us would have had numerous questions for Mary.

Instead, with the presence of the Holy Spirit, Elisabeth's vision toward Mary's situation was clear. Therefore, there was no place for ridicule or scorn. There was only the occasion for love and comradery.

Women of God, we have the indwelling of the Holy Spirit. Therefore, we should be able to respond to our sisters the same way Elisabeth responded to and received Mary. We should be able to smile in women's faces and smile behind their backs as well, instead of gossiping and spreading rumors. This is what the love of the Lord will cause us to do.

Scenario #4- Ruth and Naomi

The next example of love and understanding is the one that existed between Naomi and Ruth. First, let me provide the back story of these two women to explain how they came into each other's lives. Naomi was living in Bethlehem with her husband Elimelech and their two sons. A famine hit their land, so they were required to flee in search of food and shelter. Elimelech took his family to Moab. There, the two sons of Elimelech and Naomi married Moabite women: Ruth and Orpah.

Years later, Elimelech and the two sons died, leaving Naomi and her two daughters-in-law alone. Eventually, Naomi received word that Bethlehem had begun to prosper, and she desired to return home, to her land and to her people. She told her daughters-in-law of her plan to return to Bethlehem and recommended they return to their families. After some discussion, Orpah took Ruth's advice and went her way. However, Ruth disagreed. Ruth gave Naomi a heartfelt plea: *"Intreat me not to leave thee, or to return from following after thee: for whither thou goest, I will go; and where thou lodgest, I will lodge: thy people shall be my people, and thy God my God: Where thou diest, will I die, and there will I be buried: the Lord do so to me, and more also, if ought but death part thee and me"* (Ruth 1:16-17).

Naomi relented on the advice she had given to the two young women and allowed Ruth to travel with her back to Bethlehem. Now, let's fast forward to get to the heart of their relationship.

When Naomi returned home, she and Ruth had to feed themselves. Naomi recalled a wealthy kinsman of her husband whose name was Boaz. She obviously told Ruth about him and his field, from which the less fortunate were permitted to glean. Naomi was up in age, so Ruth took the responsibility to go out and find nourishment for the two of them. She said to Naomi, *"Let me now go to the field, and glean ears of corn after him in whose sight I shall find grace"* (Ruth 2:2a). Naomi responded, *"Go, my daughter"* (Ruth 2:2b).

When Ruth had married Naomi's son, she had become Naomi's daughter, and the relationship had not changed even after the son died. Naomi continued to embrace Ruth, and with that came training. As time progressed, Naomi provided Ruth with a set of instructions that would endear her to Boaz, especially after he had seen Ruth's treatment and respect for her mother-in-law Naomi (Ruth 2:11).

In Ruth 3:3-4, Naomi gives Ruth specific instructtions: *"Wash thyself therefore, and anoint thee, and put thy raiment upon thee, and get thee down to the floor: but make not thyself known unto the man, until he shall have done eating and drinking. And it shall be, when he lieth down, that thou shalt mark the place where he shall lie, and thou shalt go in, and uncover his feet, and lay thee down; and he will tell thee what thou shalt do."*

Ruth followed Naomi's advice to the letter and because she did, Boaz and Ruth ended up getting married and having at least one child: a son they named Obed. Naomi had lost her two sons long ago, but then, after the birth of Obed, she had a child to care for. Although Obed was not her biological grandchild, she loved him just the same.

In Naomi and Ruth's relationship, there was an older woman and a younger woman. The older woman took the younger woman under her wing. Although Naomi did not have physical wealth to give Ruth, she had a wealth of experience and knowledge to share. From all accounts, Naomi had an open heart and was willing to pour out to Ruth, who was willing to receive. Mentoring someone, training her to follow a productive path, is love poured out in abundance. This is what Naomi did for Ruth. As a result, Ruth's life was fuller, having the abundance of love and the fruitfulness of a family.

Women of God, we too can share the same love illustrated by Elisabeth and Naomi, rather than the displays of superiority, strife and hatred demonstrated by Peninnah and Hagar. Destructive spirits tear down a person's psyche and self-esteem. Love, joy, peace, longsuffering, gentleness, goodness, faith, meekness, and temperance usher in positivity, hope, encouragement, high self-esteem, self-worth, love, and kindness.

We have to be willing to look past another women's immaturity (both spiritual and psychological) and love her through the growing pains. It may take some growing on our parts before we can operate effectively in our emotions and behaviors, but if we put our minds to it and remain steadfast, we will be successful.

The success we gain in treating one another in love will eventually permeate throughout the Church. Use the following steps to increase your spiritual maturity, so you can walk fully in love and begin to eradicate negative thought and behavior patterns. Spiritual maturity is essential to overcoming the problem discussed throughout this book. Without spiritual maturity, we will all remain spiritually stunted, thereby, stunting the growth of the Body of Christ.

Step One- Activate and grow your faith. Romans 10:17 says, *"So then faith cometh by hearing, and hearing by the word of God."* The Word must constantly be in our ears, so our faith can increase.

Use II Peter 1:5-7 for Steps 2-8. *"And beside this, giving all diligence, add to your faith virtue; and to virtue knowledge; And to knowledge temperance; and to temperance patience; and to patience godliness; And to godliness brotherly kindness; and to brotherly kindness charity [love]."*

Step Two- Add virtue to your faith. Virtue is exhibiting behavior indicative of high moral standards.

Step Three- Add knowledge to virtue. To have knowledge of God's Word, you must engage with the Word, by reading your Bible, hearing the preached Word, and by engaging in Bible study.

Step Four- Add self-control to knowledge. Have you heard the phrase, "When you know better, you should do better"? The knowledge you gain from God's Word will allow you to make better choices about which words you allow to pass through your lips and how you behave.

Step Five- Add perseverance to self-control. Persevere in the will of God. Lean not to your own understanding (Proverbs 3:5-6).

Step Six- Add godliness to perseverance. Take on God's character. *"Ye shall be holy: for I the Lord your God am holy"* (Leviticus 2:19b).

Step Seven- Add brotherly kindness to godliness. Operate within the Great Commandment: *"Thou shalt love thy neighbour as thyself"* Matthew 22:39.

Step Eight- Add love to brotherly kindness. *"So now faith, hope, and love abide, these three; but the greatest of these is love"* (I Corinthians 13:13, ESV).

Navigate through the steps as you grow in the grace of God (II Peter 3:18). If you ever feel it is not worth it or that it lacks importance, think about your responsibility as a believer to advance the Kingdom of God. That in and of itself should propel you to growth, and in doing so, the Body of Christ can and will be the Church without spot, wrinkle or blemish that Jesus is coming back for (Ephesians 5:27).

Gift of Salvation for Non-Believers

"For all have sinned, and come short
of the glory of God."
(Romans 3:23)

This section was written especially for non-believers, those who have not accepted the gift of salvation. The gift of salvation saves souls from eternal damnation and is a free gift offered by God Himself.

John 3:16-18 says, *"For God so loved the world, that he gave his only begotten Son, that whosoever believeth in him should not perish, but have everlasting life. For God sent not his Son into the world to condemn the world; but that the world through him might be saved. He that believeth on him is not condemned: but he that believeth not is condemned already, because he hath not believed in the name of the only begotten Son of God."*

This section of scripture tells us God's purpose for giving His son Jesus to the world. The world was in a bad condition. The world was overwrought with sin; the people were living for fleshly desires rather than for God's desires.

As a result of the world's conditions, God decided He would offer the perfect sacrifice that would save the world from being a place where people were lost and had no hope. He decided that His own son could stand in proxy for the sin-filled world, taking all sin upon Himself.

So Jesus came, born of a virgin, to save this dying world. He walked on this earth for 33 ½ years, doing the work of His

Heavenly Father. At the appointed time, He died by way of crucifixion upon a cross at Calvary, on Golgotha's hill. He shed his blood and died for you and for me. Because His blood was pure, it paid the penalty for all unrighteousness and gave those who believe in Him direct access to His father's throne.

Scripture tells us in Matthew 27:51 that the veil of the temple was ripped in two from top to bottom, at the moment that Jesus' spirit left His body. As a result of the veil's removal, we are no longer required to have a high priest make intercession for us. We, as the children of the Most High God, are able to approach the throne of God for ourselves, and Jesus sits on the right hand of the Father making intercession for us.

But what is even more miraculous than God offering His own son as the perfect sacrifice was the fact that when Jesus was placed in grave clothes and placed in a tomb, He only remained there until the third day. God would not have it that His son would remain in the heart of the earth forever. In order for people to believe in the awesome power of God and His dear son Jesus, a miracle had to be performed. So, on the third day, after Jesus died on the cross, He was resurrected, demonstrating the omnipotence of God. This very act was the act that would cause people to believe in a god that reigns supreme and holds the power of the universe in His very hands, a god that could save them from themselves.

Today, if you are an unbeliever, you can change your destiny. You can change where you will spend your eternity. Our Heavenly Father gives us the freedom of choice about how we want to live our life here on earth and how we want to spend eternity. In Deuteronomy 30:19, God boldly declares, *"I call heaven and earth to record this day against you, that I have set before you life and death, blessing and cursing: therefore choose life, that both thou and thy seed may live."*

So, dear friend what choice will you make today? Will you spend your eternity with the Creator or will you suffer Hell's eternal flames? Again, the choice is yours. Just as the men aboard the ship who were with Jonah became believers, you too can make a choice to accept the only one and true living God as your god.

If after reading the above passages, you have decided that you want to spend your eternity in Heaven with God, the creator, and His son Jesus, and the Holy Spirit, read through what has affectionately come to be known as the Roman's Road. This is the road to salvation. As you read through the scriptures that comprise the Roman's Road, you will also read the explanation for each scripture so you will have clarity about what you are reading and confessing.

The Roman's Road to Salvation

The road to salvation begins with Romans 3:23 which declares, *"For all have sinned, and come short of the glory of God."* This scripture explains that everyone has come short of God's glory and needs redemption. Then Romans 6:23a states, *"For the wages of sin is death."* Here, we learn that the consequence of living a life of sin is death. Everyone will experience physical death as a result of the sin committed in the garden of Eden, but those who commit themselves to a life of sin will suffer eternal damnation in the lake of fire (Rev. 19).

Continue with the rest of verse 6:23 that says, *"but the gift of God is eternal life through Jesus Christ our Lord."* There is an alternative to suffering eternal damnation. We can accept the gift of salvation by accepting Jesus as our personal lord and savior. Then, Romans 5:8 says, *"But God commendeth his love toward us, in that, while we were yet sinners, Christ died for us.*" We are able to receive the gift of salvation because Christ came to earth and shed His blood for us on the cross.

Continue to Romans 10: 9-10 which says, "*That if thou shalt confess with thy mouth the Lord Jesus, and shalt believe in thine heart that God hath raised him from the dead, thou shalt be saved. For with the heart man believeth unto righteousness; and with the mouth confession is made unto salvation.*" If we confess with our mouths that Jesus is the son of God, that he came and died for our sins, and that God raised Him from the dead, we will receive salvation.

Finish with Romans 10:13, which states, "*For whosoever shall call upon the name of the Lord shall be saved.*" Call upon the name of God by saying these words, "Lord Jesus, come into my heart and save me Lord. I believe that you are the Son of God who came and died on the cross for my sins. I believe that you rose from the grave. I also believe that you now sit in heaven on the right side of the Father, making intersession for me. I accept you as my Lord and my Savior."

Now that you have confessed with your mouth that Jesus is the son of God and that He died for our sins and rose from the grave, YOU ARE NOW SAVED!!!! You will spend your eternity in heaven.

The next step is very important- you must find a Bible-based church that teaches the word of God and confesses the Lord Jesus Christ to be the son of God. Don't delay. Do this immediately. Do not leave yourself open to the enemy. Get connected with the saints of the Most High God and keep yourself covered with the unspotted blood of the lamb.

Here is my prayer for you.

Father God,

I thank you for the opportunity to minister your Word to the unsaved, the unchurched, and the uncommitted. Father God, I pray now for the souls who have just received the gift of salvation. Lord Father, they have opened their hearts to you, and I know that you have received them into your kingdom and written their names in the Book of Life. Father God, I pray that you will touch their lives and show yourself mightily before them. Let their eyes be opened by the scales falling off, allowing them to see clearly.

Father God, I even pray for the backslider, those who have turned away from you after receiving the gift of salvation. You said in your word that you desire that none would perish. So Lord, I send your word to them right now praying that they would confess the iniquity in their heart, repent, and turn from their evil ways, so that they may receive a life of abundance. You said in your word in Matthew Chapter 14, that every knee shall bow before you and every tongue will confess that Jesus is Lord.

Father God, I pray now that we all come under subjection to your word and that we will humbly submit our lives to you. I ask all these things in the name of my Lord and Savior Jesus Christ.

Amen, Amen, Amen!!!!

I will continue to pray for your success in your walk with God. Remember, this spiritual walk that you are about to embark on will not be an easy walk, but remember, the race is not given to the swift but to those who endure to the end.

Be blessed with heaven's best. I love you!

About the Author

Dr. Cassundra White-Elliott resides in California with her family, where as an English/Education professor she works for various community colleges and universities.

When writing, she writes with the direction of the Holy Spirit, in an effort to share with God's people all that He has for them.

In addition to teaching and writing, Dr. White-Elliott also serves as an evangelistic teacher. She is also the founder of International Women's Commission, a ministry that serves the needs of the entire person, by attending to healing the mind, body, soul, and spirit.

Dr. White-Elliott holds a Ph.D. in Education, a Master's in English Composition, and a Bachelor's in Education.

Dr. White-Elliott is also the founder of CLF Publishing, LLC. For your publishing needs, go online to www.clfpublishing.org.

OTHER BOOKS BY THE AUTHOR

(All books can be purchased at
www.amazon.com
www.barnesandnoble.com
www.creativemindsbookstore.com)

From Despair, through Determination, to Victory!

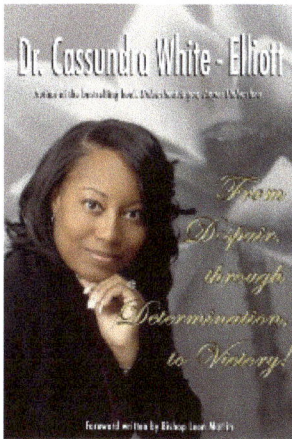

A lot can happen during a span of 40 years. The life of Dr. Cassundra White-Elliott has been anything but uneventful. From a fun-loving childhood sprinkled with incidents of abuse to a tumultuous young adulthood to a stable, secure adult life, she has experienced a full life, with much more to come. Her story is inspiring and motivating.

If anyone lacks hope, reading Dr. White-Elliott's autobiography will propel him/her into an attitude of "Maybe I can." This attitude, if nurtured and developed, will grow into an attitude of "Yes, I can." Throughout her life, Cassundra has always held in her heart the belief that she could achieve anything that she had a made-up mind to embark upon. She was determined to achieve her heart's desires, doing what God has called her to do. She takes no credit for herself. All the glory goes to God, for He is her driving force. In Him, she lives, moves, and has her being.

Through the Storm

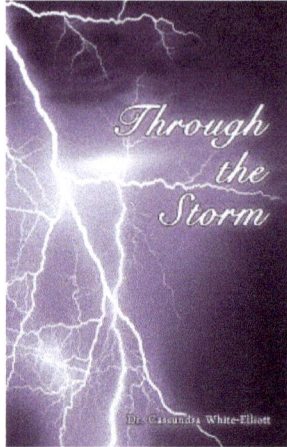

Through the Storm was duly inspired by the avaricious cloud of depression that decided to hover overhead of my daily existence in the latter part of 2007. Although I found it extremely difficult, I was once again compelled to not be defeated by just another snare that the enemy, the trickster, set for me. Once again, or more appropriately I should say *continuously*, he has exerted pernicious efforts to snatch the very life out of me by causing me to wallow in despair and to believe that I had been overcome by failure when in actuality and all reality, I was just experiencing a temporary setback. During those cloudy days, I had to remind myself daily that even though I was a target of the enemy, I am and will always be a child of the Most High god, Jehovah, who is my rock, my stability.

Unleashed Anger, Anger Unleashed

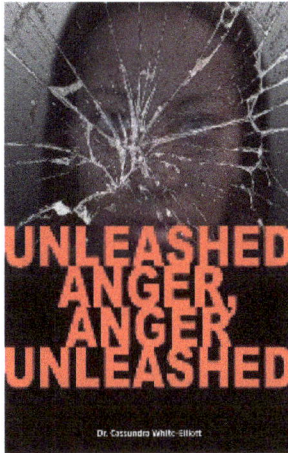

As I prepared to embark upon the adventure of writing this book, I had to prepare myself to also be transparent. I have found that being transparent is required in order for healing to transpire, healing for all those that peruse the pages of this book and myself. And I may as well tell you that today, at the onset of this project, I have not been totally delivered from my condition of being an anger-filled person. However, I am definitely a work in progress. I have made strides with the assistance of my Lord and Savior, Jesus Christ, who is the head of my life. Without his love, guidance, and teachings, I would not be the woman of God I am today. I shudder to think where I could be instead and will therefore not entertain the thought.

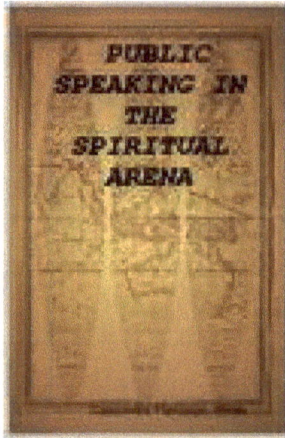

Chapter Two
How Communication Works
Purpose: This chapter will explain the six primary components of communication, identifying their purpose and how they work together.

The Source

In oral communication, the source of information is the speaker. In a church setting, the foundation of the message is God's word, but it is a speaker's interpretation of God's word that is delivered to the audience. As speakers vary, the information may vary but should have a similar essence because the foundational text is the same.

The Message

The message is the collective set of ideas that the speaker (the source) wants to deliver and/or illustrate to the audience.

Where is Your Joppa?

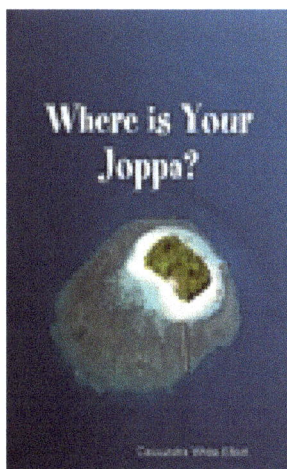

Introduction

Where is Your Joppa? was written for the express purpose of illustrating God's call for obedience in the lives of believers with respect to the individual call that He has on each of our lives. As you read throughout the various chapters, notice that the emphasis is placed on our persistent disobedience in answering God's call in a specific area of our lives. We have become a people who are similar to the Israelites when they found themselves in the middle of the wilderness, following their exodus from Egypt. Before God, they murmured and complained about their current life conditions and failed to be obedient to God's statutes delivered through His servant Moses. Their persistent disobedience caused them to lose the opportunity to see and enter the Promised Land. I ask you, "What has your disobedience cost you?" "Was your disobedience worth what it cost you?" "Do you think about the souls you could have ushered into the kingdom of God?" These are some of the questions that I pray will be answered through your reading of the book.

Mayhem in the Hamptons

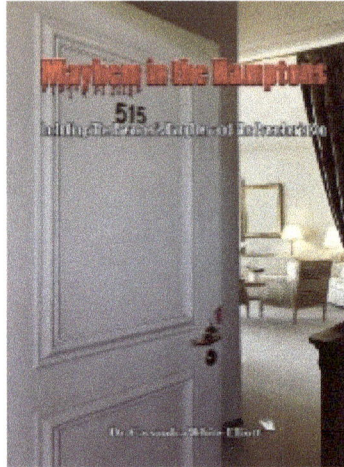

Romero and Yolanda optimistically plan for the day that is going to change their lives from being single persons to a couple who is united in holy matrimony. They, along with their parents, close friends and family, fly over to the infamous Hamptons, where only the rich and famous vacation, to have their dream wedding at the five-star Hampton Suites located on a peninsula in the Hamptons. Little do they know that their perfect day will turn out to be less than perfect when their wedding planner Mariesha Coleman suddenly goes missing!

A time when the newlyweds' lives should be filled with joy and the creation of wonderful memories, they are stricken with grief as they desperately try to find clues to help solve Mariesha's disappearance.

Mayhem in the Hamptons is a tale that shares how the horrors of a woman's past can come back to haunt her in more than one way and the impact it can have on anyone who gets in the way.

Preacher's Daughter

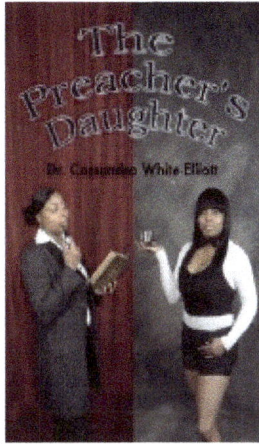

Tinisha, the daughter of a preacher, is a twenty-six year-old God-fearing young woman endeavoring to complete law school so that she can make her mark in the courtroom. Working in one of the late-night clubs in Hollywood to earn money to pay her own way through school, Tinisha soon learns that life doesn't always go as planned.

Preacher's Son

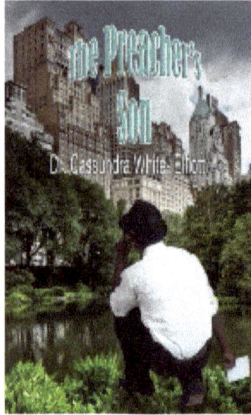

Romero Turner is a private investigator with a promising future. As he continues to build his career, he is excited about the cases he undertakes. However, his father Pastor Theodore Turner has other plans for his son's life. In the midst of trying to save his client's husband from Sylvester Domingo, a ruthless crime lord, Romero must try to salvage his relationship with his father. He must decide if ministry or life as a detective is in his future.

Lord, Teach Me to be a Blessing!

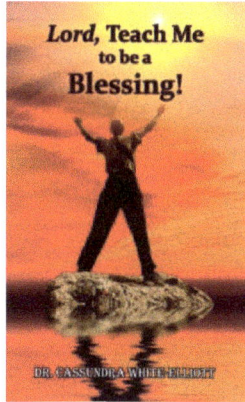

Lord, Teach Me to be a Blessing! will change a person's mentality from being centered around "me, myself, and I" to focusing on "others."

The world system teaches us that it is acceptable to place ourselves above others in an attempt to get ahead and even to survive. Herbert Spencer coined the phrase '*survival of the fittest*' after reading Charles Darwin's theory of evolution. This concept of surpassing and outdoing others is the world's philosophy.

However, the word of God does not subscribe to or promote this self-centered ideology, and therefore, neither should believers. We must hold fast to the truths outlined in Scrip-ture: "*Love thy neighbor as you love thyself.*"

After the Dust Settles

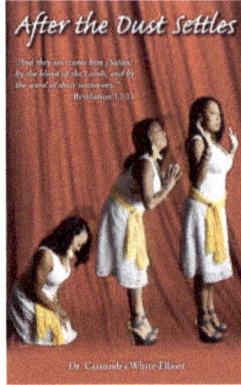

Throughout the journey of life, we all experience ups and downs and joys and pains. Most of us successfully find solutions to the situations/problems we encounter, but we often avoid dealing with the attached emotions. If we continue to ignore the emotions of pain, hurt, disappointment, anger, etc., we set ourselves up for destruction. Our families, our cultures, and our society tell us to be strong, to keep our chin up, and to grin and bear it. However, these methods of avoidance can lead us to strokes due to the undue amount of pressure we place on ourselves and/or mental illness from being unable to cope with the emotional baggage we have accumulated.

A Diamond in the Rough

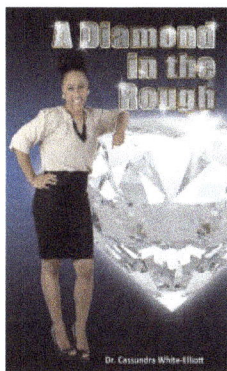

A Diamond in the Rough Architecture Firm was built and is owned and operated by lead architect Kyra Fraser. For the last five years, Kyra has been extremely successful in business, but her love life leaves much to be desired.

Kyra has set high standards for herself and does not wish to take a man in any condition and attempt to make him over. She is looking for someone who is drama free, well educated, very cultured, fun-loving, good looking, self-motivated, and the list goes on.

Will Kyra find the man of her dreams, or will her dream just continue to be a dream?

As you delve into this page-turning novel, Kyra's reality will unfold as you are drawn into her world of design, love and office drama- which includes her best friend's husband who is looking for love in all the wrong places.

365 Days of Encouragement

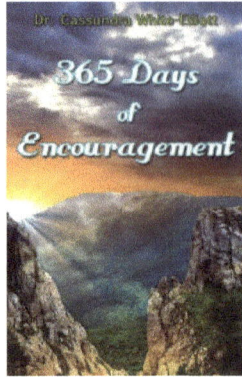

Just as our brain requires oxygen obtained from the air we breathe to sustain our mortal bodies, our spirit requires revitalization and encouragement in order to be strengthened each and every day of our lives. The revitalization and encouragement needed for the spirit of man comes directly from the word of God and assists us in walking according to the way of our heavenly Father. 365 Days of Encouragement provides a scripture a day for each day of the year. Along with the daily scripture is a brief note of commentary also for the benefit of edifying the saints of God.

It is my prayer that the people of God would live a fulfilled life through Christ Jesus. Knowing His word and understanding we can walk in the fulfillment thereof is empowering.

A Mother's Heart

A Mother's Heart shares the unconditional love of mothers through a compilation of testimonies. Each testimony serves as a tribute to a special mother. The children of the represented mothers have lovingly written about their childhood, young adult life and/or older adult experiences they shared with their mother. As you read the writers' reflections, you will feel the expressions of love exude from the pages.

Our advice to mothers is, "Be encouraged; the journey of motherhood may seem daunting at times and you may shed some tears, but your children will never forget the love you have shown them and instilled in them to share with others."

Broken Chains

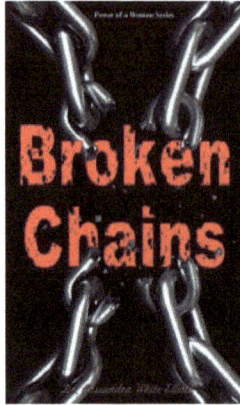

Broken Chains is an in-depth survey of five life-changing tragedies that can and will serve as chains to bind us if we are not watchful and mindful of their potential effects. In our lifetimes, we may all experience death of loved ones, sexual abuse, broken relationships, promiscuity, and sickness and disease. These everyday life occurrences can have detrimental effects on the remaining years of our lives and change our existence, unless we deal with them in a healthy manner.

Broken Chains not only brings to light the detrimental effects of five life-changing tragedies, but it also shares how anyone who experiences them can be healed and delivered from their effects.

I Have Fallen

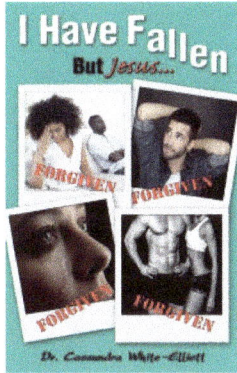

Do you know anyone who has committed his/her life to Christ but has done something unseemly that you would never expect a Christian to do? How did you feel about that person or what the person did? Did you pass judgment? What if that person were you? How would you feel if you made a misstep and no one forgave you and instead began to treat you differently? How do you feel when you are judged for past mistakes or lifestyles that are no longer part of your life?

This book shares four true stories of Christians who have made missteps during their walk with God. The purpose is not to air their dirty laundry, but to demonstrate our humanness and our vulnerability. None of us are exempt from making errors and falling into sin. It can happen to any of us.

The Bottom Line

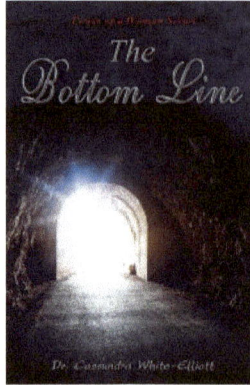

The Bottom Line is a detailed review of the Book of Job. Much can be said about Job's experiences with the loss of his children and wealth and the subsequent return of it all in mass proportions. However, the telling of Job's story in the Holy writ was not intended to focus on the return of his wealth. Instead, the focal point should be on the bottom line of the entire situation.

When you experience trials or tragedies in your life, do you tend to focus on the trial itself, the result, or the bottom line? "What is the bottom line?" you may ask. The bottom line is the message God is sending regarding the situation.

Power of a Woman

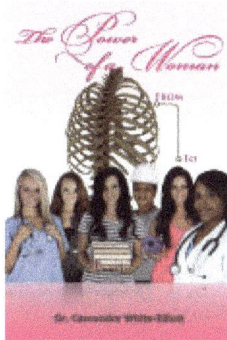

The ongoing conversation about the value of a woman is presented from a different perspective in *The Power of a Woman*. Dr. Cassundra White-Elliott presents a biblical perspective of women and compares it to the worldview of both yesterday and today. This comparison seeks to illustrate God's intended purpose for His uniquely designed creation: woman. Dr. Elliott shares God's truth about pre-imposed limitations set by man versus the limitations God Himself set for woman in addition to the wealth of liberality He gave her. Women, let's take the blinders off, lift our heads up, and march forward, side by side with men, and bring glory and honor to God! Take your rightful place with a gentle smile and grace and be who God called you to be!

Set Free

If you possess habits and display characteristics that are unbecoming, debilitating, and hinder the desired progress in your life or that affect your relationships with others, Set Free will provide the steps you need to be healed and delivered, through the Word of God.

Deliverance is available to you! Claim your healing today and walk in victory!

Do You Know God?

Have you or someone you know ever felt alone, confused, or unsure about your walk with God or are you unsure of what being a Christian is all about? *Do You Know God?* is an excellent text for providing answers to many of your questions. This book introduces adolescents and young adults to God in addition to answer many of their questions about being a Christian. This book shares the testimonies of the trials and tribulations that other teens have experienced and how God prevailed in their lives. All the information that is shared on the pages of the book is based upon the Word of God and the scriptures are taken from the King James Version of the Bible. If you are interested in knowing more about God's Word or how to begin your Christian experience, this book is for you.

Daughter, God Loves You!

"...for her price is far above rubies."
(Proverbs 31:10b)

Dr. Cassundra White-Elliott

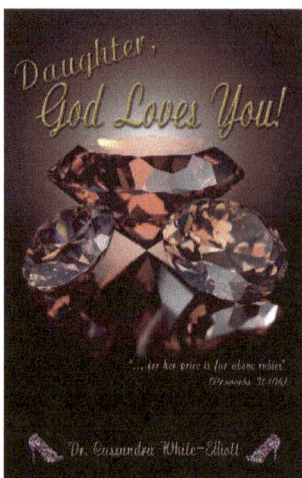

Maybe you have heard the proclamation, "The world is going to hell in a hand basket!" Well, I believe I must concur.

However, I do *not* believe, we- the adult, mature believers- should sit idly by and allow our daughters (and our sons for that matter) to go with it! We must fight for our girls and young women, for they are the mothers of tomorrow, and some may even be young mothers today. Not only will they continue the human race, but also they can have bright futures in their careers and as leaders in our society, as they allow God to direct their paths and order their steps.

Daughter, God Loves You! is an earnest attempt to address many of the issues that plague our society and turn our daughters' heads away from God.

In this book, we dive head first into topics such as God's love, the importance and impact of education, the effects of social media, overcoming abuse, and the proper perspective of the future.

For the young adult women- Reading this book will empower you to have a bright prosperous future from being enlightened about the dangers that plague our society and how to avoid pitfalls, as you walk along the path God has paved for you.

I invite all of you to take this journey with me to save our daughters and yourselves (young women) from corruption, by being empowered with knowledge.

We must thwart the plan of the enemy. So, LET'S GO!

CLF Publishing, LLC.
www.clfpublishing.org

Dr. C. White-Elliott's books are available at:
www.creativemindsbookstore.com
www.amazon.com
www.barnesandnoble.com

ISBN 978-0-9961971-9-9

9 780996 197199

90000

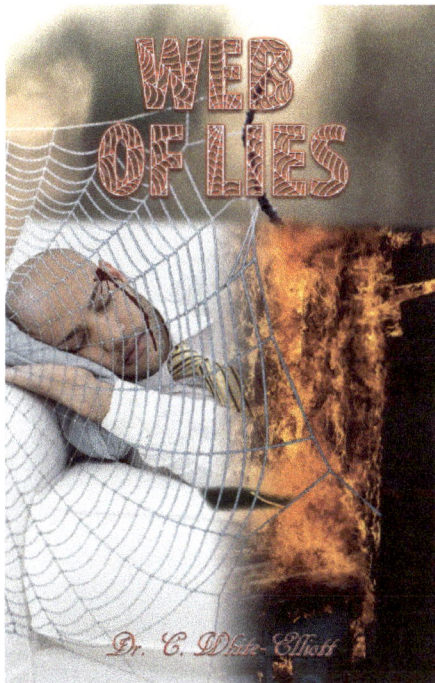

WEB OF LIES

Dr. C. Wade-Elliott

A year ago, Charlito Jimenez was found in his den, lying on the couch, with a fatal gunshot wound in his temple.

Everyone in the community still wants to know who is guilty of the unfathomable crime.

Tinisha Salisbury, attorney at law, has taken the case of the accused. Can she prove her client's innocence or will a guilty verdict be rendered?

Halfway through the trial, a badly burned body was found at the scene of a fire.

Is there a string of murders being committed?

Are the murders related?

Web of Lies spins the tales of several characters into one web. Each has a story to tell, and everyone has something to hide. The web of lies, deceit, and revenge take over the lives of these characters to the point where they may not be able to see their way clear.

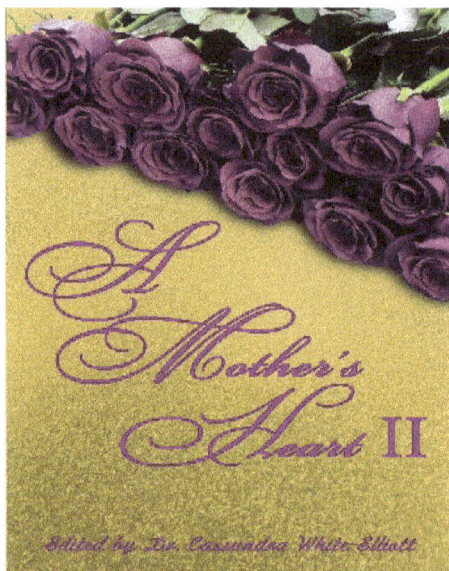

A Mother's Heart II shares the unconditional love of mothers through a compilation of testimonies. Each testimony serves as a tribute to a special mother. The children of the represented mothers have lovingly written about their childhood, young adult life and/or older adult experiences they shared with their mother. As you read the writers' reflections, you will feel the expressions of love exude from the pages.

The purpose of this book is two-fold. First, it honors those mothers who stood by their children through the trials of life and showered them with unconditional love. Second, the book is a source of encouragement for mothers who may feel inadequate and question whether or not they are actually suited for motherhood. Our advice to mothers is, *"Be encouraged; the journey of motherhood may seem daunting at times and you may shed some tears, but your children will never forget the love you have shown them and instilled in them to share with others."*

Mothers may not be perfect, but they are definitely unmatched by any other category of person on God's green earth!

The following authors are included in this compilation:
Edwin Baltierra, Shelia Bryant-Colbert, Jean Cedeno,
Ilse Guadalupe Hernandez, Haley Keil, Haley King, Johnathon Lopez,
Ronnette Moore, Allyson Marie Sanders, Lucas van den Elzen,
Daron C. White, Ashton Wilson, Jessica Yslas, and Vanessa Zavala

CLF Publishing, LLC.
www.clfpublishing.org

Dr. Cassundra White-Elliott's books are available at:
www.creativemindsbookstore.com
www.amazon.com
www.barnesandnoble.com

ISBN 978-1-945102-02-8
90000
9 781945 102028

Power of a Woman Series

Embracing Womanhood
The Journey of a Queen

"But ye are a chosen generation, a royal priesthood, an holy nation, a peculiar people..." 1 Peter 2:9

Dr. Cassandra White-Elliott

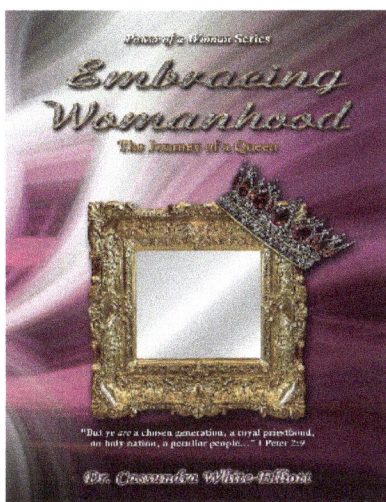

The journey from adolescence through puberty to young adulthood can be challenging and quite disconcerting for the average young lady. The changes that occur both mentally and physically can be both confusing and uncomfortable. However, the outcome of the changes can be beautiful. What she will experience during this time in her life is simply a metamorphosis – taking off the old and embracing the new. The process is similar to that of an awkward caterpillar that overtime develops into a beautiful, graceful butterfly.

The topics covered in this book (puberty, self esteem, mental stability, goals, finances, and relationships) will assist young women (ages 15–23) in understanding the transformation they are enduring to prepare them for the life that lies ahead. After taking in the information, they will literally witness themselves evolve from princess to queen!

CLF Publishing, LLC.
www.clfpublishing.org

Dr. Cassandra White-Elliott's books are available at:
www.creativemindsbookstore.com
www.amazon.com
www.barnesandnoble.com

ISBN 978-1-945102-13-8

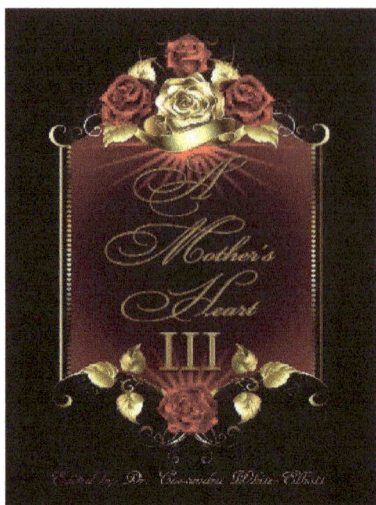

A Mother's Heart III shares the unconditional love of mothers through a compilation of testimonies. Each testimony serves as a tribute to a special mother. The children of the represented mothers have lovingly written about their childhood, young adult life and/or older adult experiences they shared with their mother. As you read the writers' reflections, you will feel the expressions of love exude from the pages.

The purpose of this book is two fold. First, it honors those mothers who stood by their children through the trials of life and showered them with unconditional love. Second, the book is a source of encouragement for mothers who may feel inadequate and question whether or not they are actually suited for motherhood.

Our advice to mothers is, "Be encouraged; the journey of motherhood may seem daunting at times and you may shed some tears, but your children will never forget the love you have shown them and instilled in them to share with others." Mothers may not be perfect, but they are definitely unmatched by any other category of person on God's green earth!

The following authors are included in this compilation:
Yolanda Castro, Georgette Utz, Isaac Thompson, Nicholas Harrison,
Justin Harrison, Ashleigh Morris, Jerry G. Martin, Jourdan Jover,
Khalil Fleurister, Audrey Albrecht, Caray Vines-Nichols, Acayla Clayton,
Delevian Jackson, Quantunique Williams, Millicent Redd, Ahleeyah Nichols,
Julia Lacy, Maria Guzman, Tyler Kowalski-Foley, Haley Kril,
Fernando Lescano, Elaine M. Tolentino and Karen Ruiz.

CLF Publishing, LLC.
www.clfpublishing.org

Dr. Cassandra White-Elliott's books are available at:
www.creativemindsbookstore.com
www.amazon.com
www.barnesandnoble.com

ISBN 978-1-945102-16-5
90000

9 781945 102165

The Making of
Dr. C.
A Memoir

The Making of Dr. C. shares the 50-year journey of Dr. Cassundra White-Elliott. Her journey of trials, missteps, successes, and triumphs will inspire you to face any trial you may encounter with a positive attitude and the Word of God.

Her life demonstrates no matter what you may face, there is always a brighter tomorrow.

Keeping the faith will allow God to work in your life. After all, He only wants the best for you!

CLF Publishing, LLC.
www.clfpublishing.org

Dr. Cassundra White-Elliott's books are available at:
www.creativemindsbookstore.com
www.amazon.com
www.barnesandnoble.com

ISBN 978-1-945102-32-5
90000
9 781945 102325

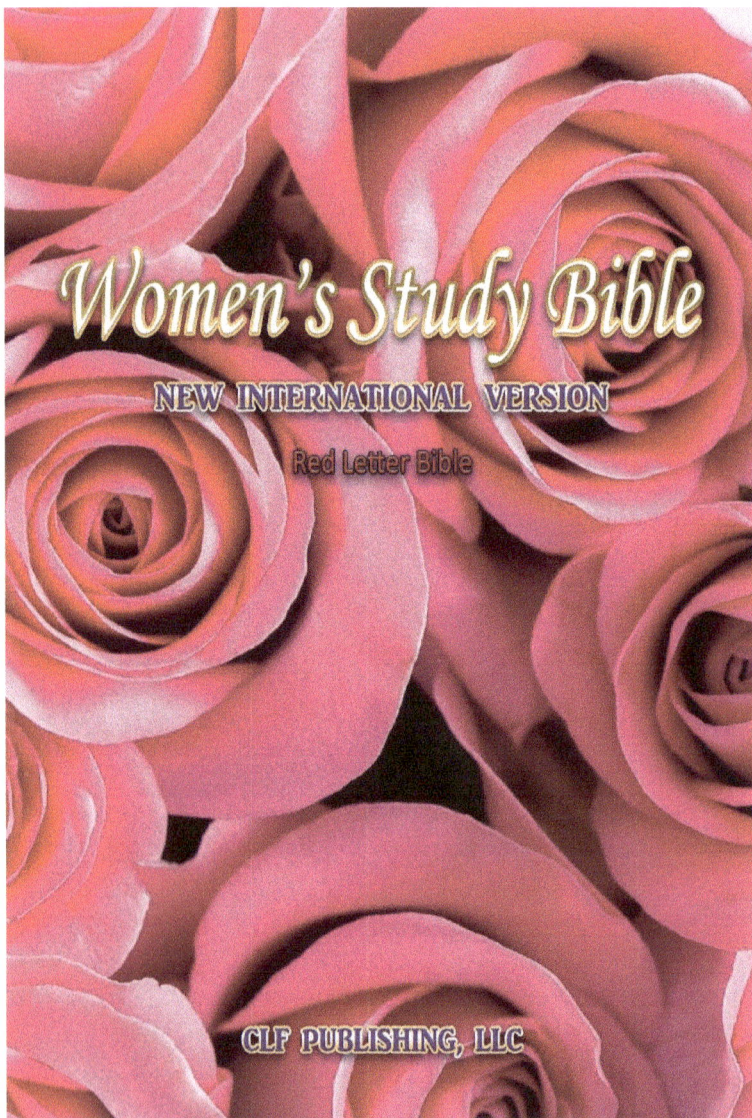

Women's Study Bible

NEW INTERNATIONAL VERSION

Red Letter Bible

CLF PUBLISHING, LLC

Power of a Woman Series

CLAIM *Your*

Luci Brigli Rani Marisol Tracy

INHERITANCE

Dr. Cassundra White-Elliott

"The thief cometh not, but for to steal, and to kill, and to destroy: I am come that they might have life, and that they might have it more abundantly" (John 10:10).

*S*atan's mission is to steal, kill, and destroy all that God has provided for us. With him on the rampage, we must be ready to go to war- spiritually and naturally. On the other hand, we could sit idly by and allow the enemy to take what is rightfully ours. However, that is not the will of God. God has given us power to tread upon serpents and scorpions (Luke 10:19) and to reclaim all the enemy has stolen from us.

This book will share how we can be victorious in reclaiming what is rightfully ours when the enemy has turned his ugly head in our direction and made us prey for his latest scheme.

With God on our side, the enemy will not prevail!

CLF Publishing, LLC.
www.clfpublishing.org

Dr. Cassundra White-Elliott's books are available at:
www.creativemindsbookstore.com • www.amazon.com • www.barnesandnoble.com

ISBN 978-1-945102-33-2
90000
9 781945 102332

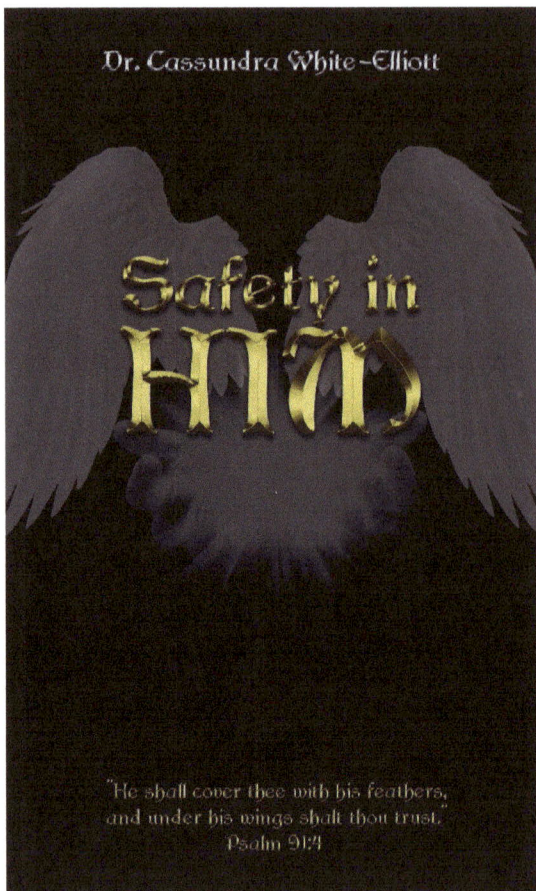

Dr. Cassundra White-Elliott

Safety in יהוה

"He shall cover thee with his feathers,
and under his wings shalt thou trust."
Psalm 91:4

In this book, particular attention is brought to Psalm 91:1-7. In these verses, God promises His divine protection for His children. Read Christopher's story and see how the divine protective nature of God is demonstrated and remember Acts 10:34b, which states, *"God is no respecter of persons."* What He is able to do for one, He is able to do for another. So, no matter what you be faced with today, call on the Lord, and He will deliver you!

Christian Inspiration Jan 2019

Christian Inspiration April 2019

July 2019

Christian Inspiration

A Publication of CLF Publishing, LLC

ISAAC DOUGLAS
BORN TO BE A BOSS

Inside This Issue:
- ❖ Gut Health
- ❖ Setting Up a Business
- ❖ The Importance of Being Equally Yoked
- ❖ Forming a Nonprofit Organization
- ❖ Using African-American Literature to Educate

Christian Inspiration July 2019

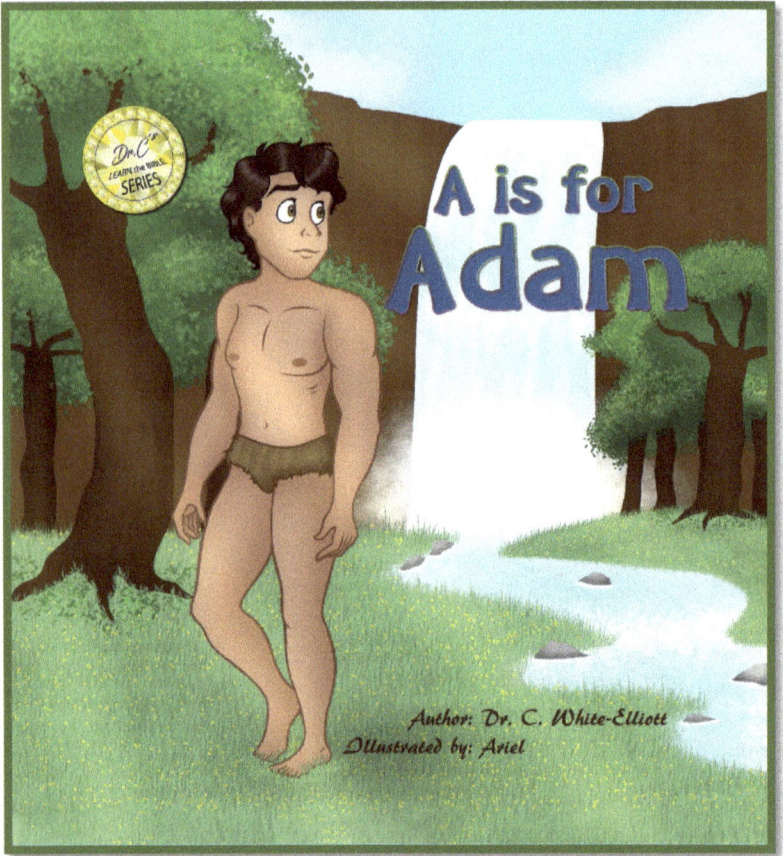

Dr. C's
LEARN THE BIBLE
SERIES

A is for
Adam

Author: Dr. C. White-Elliott
Illustrated by: Ariel

A is for Adam is a tool to teach young minds about the Word of God.

God created Adam and placed him in the Garden of Eden.

Adam named all the animals.

See if you can name them too.

Ages 2-7

www.ingramcontent.com/pod-product-compliance
Lightning Source LLC
LaVergne TN
LVHW070013090426
835508LV00048B/3383